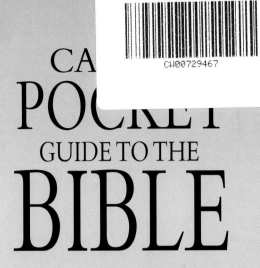

CA...
POCKET
GUIDE TO THE
BIBLE

**THE BASIC REFERENCE BOOK
FOR BIBLE STUDENTS**

William F. Kerr

CANDLE
BOOKS

Text © 2000 International Publishing,
San Dimas, CA
Copyright © 2000 Lion Hudson plc/
Tim Dowley & Peter Wyart trading as Three's
Company

Published in the UK 2004 by Candle Books
(a publishing imprint of Lion Hudson plc).
Distributed by Marston Book Services Ltd
PO Box 269, Abingdon, Oxon OX14 4YN

Originally published in 1982 as *Kerr's
Handbook to the Bible*.
Previously published in 2000 as
Student Pocket Guide to the Bible.

Designed by Peter Wyart

Worldwide coedition organised and
produced by
Lion Hudson plc, Mayfield House,
256 Banbury Road,
Oxford, OX2 7DH, England.
Tel: +44 (0) 1865 302750
Fax: +44 (0) 1865 302757
Email: coed@lionhudson.com
www.lionhudson.com

Printed in Singapore

Picture acknowledgements

Photographs
Tim Dowley: pp. 1, 17, 19, 23, 25
28, 31, 57, 61, 65, 67, 71, 77,
95, 99, 101, 103, 108, 109, 110
129, 133, 135, 149, 151, 157
Jamie Simson: pp. 131, 138, 141
Peter Wyart: pp. 3, 4, 7, 11, 13, 3
39, 63, 73, 75, 81, 85, 89, 97,
111, 113, 117, 120, 137, 147

Illustrations
Alan Harris: p. 92
James Macdonald: pp. 27, 59, 14
Richard Scott: pp. 33, 51, 53

Maps
Jeremy Gower

Contents

Preface

These simple, brief studies on the Bible are sent forth with the prayer that they will be helpful to those who seek to know God's Word. It is hoped that they will help to develop on the part of the reader a deeper desire to know God's Word better. Also I pray that the reader will submit to the divine command: "Study to show thyself approved unto God, a workman that needeth not to be ashamed, rightly dividing the word of truth" (2 Timothy 2:15).

A systematic, disciplined study time of some fifteen minutes daily, using these brief study helps and spent in the Word itself, will be of inestimable aid in gaining at least an introductory knowledge of that Book which is above all books.

In this day when the battle rages around and for the Bible, the believer needs to know the Word of God which is "honey out of the rock" and which is not only sweet to the taste but good for the soul and spirit. For as the psalmist reminds us: "For ever, O LORD, thy word is settled in heaven" (Psalm 119:89) and "Thy word is a lamp unto my feet, and a light unto my path" (Psalm 119:105), and again, "the entrance of thy words giveth light. . . ." (Psalm 119:130). For the one who wants to walk God's way, the above statements will urge a steady spiritual diet of God's Word.

In the preparation of this material, I wish to thank Dr. Richard Patterson, Professor of Old Testament at Northwest Baptist Seminary, Tacoma, Washington, for his invaluable help in reading and editing the manuscript and making a number of very important suggestions in relation to the contents.

My shortcomings in the work—and I'm sure there are many—are my responsibility alone.

William F. Kerr, Th.D., S.T.D.

The Bible

Unique among the books of the world is the Bible. The perennial best-seller, the Bible is to the believer the Holy Scriptures, the Word of God—and the wayfaring man, though he be a fool, can by reading it find the way of salvation.

The word "Bible" means book, being derived from the smaller form of *Biblios* which is *Biblion* (a little book). Hence, the Bible is *the book* of books. The story of the death of Sir Walter Scott illustrates this. When dying, Scott, the possessor of a great library, called to his son-in-law: "Bring me the book!" "Which book?" asked the son. Sir Walter Scott replied, "There is only *one* book, it is the Bible." That this book so impressed him as did no other is recorded in the poem he had already written:

Within that awful volume lies
The mystery of mysteries!
Happiest they of the human race
To whom their God has granted grace
To read, to fear, to hope, to pray,
To lift the latch, and force the way;
And better had they ne'er been born
Who read to doubt, or read to scorn.

The Bible is, indeed, unique among books and its uniqueness may be seen from the following:

1. In its source
The Bible comes not from any attempt by men to discover God and thus record their experiences with God. The Bible itself states that God is the source, the initiator of revelation. "All Scripture is given by inspiration of God. . . ." (2 Timothy 3:16). If humanity was to know anything about God, with any degree of assurance, then God must reveal himself—his nature, his claims upon men and his purpose, both in the history of humankind and in and for his own among humans. His revelation is unfolded progressively in and through historical events. Beginning with our first parents in the Garden of Eden (Genesis 1–3), his purpose is made known as he unfolds redemptive history through a cho-

sen individual—Abraham (Genesis 12–50), a chosen people—Israel (Exodus–Malachi), a chosen Redeemer—Christ (Matthew–John), a chosen body—his church (Acts–Jude), and then is consummated in his kingdom (Revelation 20) and then his heavenly state (Revelation 21–22).

2. In its style

The literary style of the Bible portrays a sublimity and unity that is startling. Men such as H. G. Wells have tried to duplicate it but have given up the attempts in hopeless frustration.

This is remarkable since the Bible was produced over a period of some fifteen centuries by a variety of authors. It consists of three different languages: Hebrew—which is the language of the bulk of the Old Testament; Aramaic—which is found in Ezra 4:8–6:18; 7:12–26; Daniel 2:4–7:28; Jeremiah 10:11; and Greek—the universal language of Christ's day and in which the entire New Testament was written. Also compounding this remarkability is the wide variety of backgrounds—from scholars to fishermen—among the human instruments God used to record his revelation.

But how could such a unity of style be attained? The Bible itself gives the reason. "For the prophecy came not in old time by the will of man: but holy men of God spake as they were moved by the Holy Ghost" (2 Peter 1:21). The Holy Spirit is the real author of the Bible and the variety of human instruments

A perennial bestseller, the Bible is to the believer the Holy Scriptures, the Word of God.

to produce it are under his guiding and guarding control (John 14:26; 15:26–27; 16:12–15; 1 Corinthians 2:7–12). Such an authorship is responsible for this unique literary style and the inability of any human author to duplicate it.

3. In its supernatural authority and inspiration

Because of the uniqueness of its source and style, there needs to be an explanation of why this book is superior to all other sacred books of competing religions which contend that they are authoritative for humankind.

Why is the Bible superior to all other sacred books and unique as a revelation of religious truth? Because it is divinely inspired. And inspiration is not accomplished in isolation.

The Context for Inspiration

a. Selection: God did not simply use any human instrument to bring into existence the Bible. Special men with the right backgrounds and qualifications were selected by God. For a book such as Genesis with its opening chapters dealing with the creation of the universe, human beings, and history, he selected a man such as Moses who "was learned in all the wisdom of the Egyptians" (Acts 7:22); a man like David—a mighty king and the sweet singer of Israel, to write the Psalms; Isaiah, related to royalty, to pen the book which bears his name; John—meditative, compassionate, devoted to God, a fisherman, to speak of God's love and the need to make people fishers of men; Paul —educated, brilliant, trained at Gamaliel's feet and the University of Tarsus, to write Romans and his other profound letters.

Without divine selection of special human instruments, there could be no supernaturally authoritative Bible.

b. Revelation: By his Holy Spirit, God revealed to these specially chosen instruments that truth—both known and unknown—which he wanted included in the Bible.

c. Inspiration: The Holy Spirit guarded and guided the human instruments so that the revealed truth which God desired was recorded in a written record. Consequently, a number of factors were involved in a process which had to take into consideration such factors as the background, preparation, personality, style of writing of the particular human author of the book. The significant fact then is the *result* of this act rather than the act itself. Hence, there is a confluence or flowing together of the influence of the Holy Spirit in his control over the human authors so that the Bible is an inspired record of divine revelation in the words of God in the languages, literary style

The Books of the Bible

The Bible is made up of a "library" of 66 books, 39 in the Old Testament, 27 in the New. The writings of the **OLD TESTAMENT** first appeared as separate scrolls in Hebrew; we do not know how or when they were first gathered into a single volume. The 39 books of the Old Testament vary in authorship and style and can be divided into four major groupings:

Law
Sometimes called the Pentateuch, or "five scrolls."

History
Tracing the story of God's people from their entry into the Promised Land to the Exile.

Poetry and Wisdom
Full of proverbs, riddles, parables, warnings and wise sayings.

Prophecy
God's prophets explained what had happened in the past; spoke out against evil in the present; and told of what God would do in the future.

The Apocrypha
The Apocrypha is a collection of books and additions to Old Testament books written between 300 B.C. and A.D. 100. It was not accepted by the Jews as part of Old Testament Scripture, and most Protestant denominations do not accept it as part of genuine Scripture.

The books are interesting and valuable historical documents that range from historical narratives to pious fiction.

The 27 books of the **NEW TESTAMENT** were written in Greek and can also be divided into different types of writing:

History
The book of Acts and the four Gospels. The Gospels, however, are not simply historical records; they were written to persuade readers to believe in Jesus and form portraits of Jesus as the Messiah.

Letters
These include Paul's letters to churches in various cities, his letters to individual Christians, and letters written by other apostles.

Revelation
This book opens with letters to seven churches in Asia Minor, but continues with vivid visions about the Last Days.

and personalities of the human authors.

Contrasting this with revelation and defining the relationship between the two, one notes that revelation is a *process* and can be described as *inflow* and *terminates* in the human author; inspiration is an *act* which is *outflow* and *terminates* in a written record. It is, therefore, the record that is inspired rather than the human instruments. In all this the Holy Spirit is the *Agent,* guiding, controlling both process and act which gives mankind an inspired Bible—a God-breathed Book—unique among all sacred books of all religious systems because of its supernatural authority and inspiration.

d. Transmission: This facet of the Bible is not in the same category as those already discussed. While the Holy Spirit so guided and controlled revelation and inspiration that the Bible is infallible (does not tend to error) and inerrant (it is without error) in the original writings as they came from the hands of the authors, he did not exercise the same kind of supervision over its transmission. And yet he exercised such a general oversight and supervision over the text that it is essentially today what it was when originally given.

That such a product is possible is the result of two basic factors:

1. The very careful preservation of the Old Testament text by the Jews who believed it to be the inspired Word of God—the very oracles of God (Romans 3:2).

2. The equally diligent efforts of scholars in textual criticism to compare the over 5,500 manuscripts of the Greek New Testament in order to arrive at as pure a text as possible.

God has carefully supervised the transmission of his Holy Word over the centuries so that today we have, in many cases in our own language, the reliable and authoritative Word of God.

The believer also can have the assurance that the Bible is the supernaturally authoritative and inspired record of God's revelation, as Paul says, by the inner witness of the Holy Spirit to his or her heart (Romans 8:14–16). The Westminster Confession expresses this idea in these words: ". . . our full persuasion and assurance of the infallible truth and divine authority thereof, is from the inward work of the Holy Spirit, bearing witness by and with the word in our hearts."

4. In its subject matter

The subject matter and the method of its treatment mark the Bible as unique. No other sacred book, among religious faiths, discusses the concepts with which mankind is concerned in the same way and in such depth as does the Bible. The three fundamental questions which face every man are answered profoundly by the Bible: From whence did I come? Who am I? What is my destiny? Beginning with Genesis and running all the way through the book of Revelation, these questions are considered and answered: Man came by direct creation of God, was placed in a perfect paradise, and fell into sin. Then God declared humanity sinful, corrupt, and unable to please him; their hearts are deceitful above all things and desperately wicked. Consequently, we cannot make ourselves right with God. Only God can redeem us and guarantee us eternal life through saving grace by the death of his own Son. The promise of redemption begins in Genesis 3:15, "And I will put enmity between thee and the woman, and between thy seed and her seed; it shall bruise thy head, and thou shalt bruise his heel" (Genesis 3:15) and continues to its consummation in Revelation 22:17, "And the Spirit and the bride say, Come. And let him that heareth say, Come. And let him that is athirst come. And whosoever will, let him take the water of life freely." Many events, consuming centuries, take place between the time of mankind's creation and fall and the event of the cross—which provides our redemption—and the revelation of God's final programme when our final destiny shall be settled—either a glorious heaven by faith in Christ or an eternal hell by rejecting God's provision of salvation (Revelation 20:14–15).

Many and varied are the subjects covered in this great drama

Jews at Jerusalem's Western Wall reading from a treasured copy of the Torah, the Books of the Law.

of salvation which answer man's profoundest questions: From whence did I come? From God's creative hand and made in God's image! Who am I? A sinner—corrupt and depraved, subject to the temptations and lusts and sins of this sinful nature but also the object of God's love! What is my destiny? As a believer—heaven; as an unbeliever—hell!

An anonymous writer has succinctly summarized that which makes the Bible the world's unique book:

"This Book contains the word of God, the state of man, the way of salvation, the doom of sinners, and the happiness of believers. Its doctrines are holy, its precepts are binding, its histories are truth, and its decisions are immutable. Read it to be wise, believe it to be safe, and practise it to be holy. It contains light to direct you, food to support you, and comfort to cheer you. It is the traveller's map, the pilgrim's staff, the pilot's compass, the soldier's sword, and the Christian's charter. Here paradise is restored, heaven opened, and the gates of hell disclosed. Christ is its grand object, our good its design, and the glory of God its end. It should fill the memory, rule the heart, and guide the feet. Read it slowly, frequently, prayerfully. It is a mine of wealth, a paradise of glory, and a river of pleasure. It is given in life, will be opened at the judgment, and be remembered forever. It involves the highest responsibility, will restore the greatest labour, and condemns all who trifle with its sacred contents."

5. In its standard as authoritative and divine

Many books of a religious nature relating to both the Old Testament and the New Testament were in existence but were not recognized as canonical and thus not included in the books which finally were collected and became what we know as the Bible today. Of course, as a result of the Council of Trent, following the Reformation, the Roman Catholic Church included those Apocryphal books which were written during the time between Malachi and the Gospels. These books were called apocryphal or "hidden" because they were not properly related to the Old Testament. They were not automatically or genuinely scriptural. They just did not possess those characteristics nor meet the "standard" which would have given them equal status with the biblical books.

This standard was conformity to two principles which, if met, would give them canonicity and they would be authoritative and divine. The word "canonicity" comes from the word "canon" which means a "rule" or "standard of measurement." Utilizing these principles: (a) that the book was written by a prophet or an apostle or by one who stood in a special relationship to such (for instance Mark and his relationship to Peter and Luke in his relationship to Paul), this principle then is known as prophetic witness or apostolic authority; (b) the inner witness of the Holy Spirit, by which the true believer has the basic conviction that the books of the Bible are indeed the very Word of God. This conviction becomes more and more settled in the believer's heart and as he or she reads competing books which are not biblical the believer rejects them.

Qumran •

Anyone who is a believer today can utilize this process and by comparing non-canonical with the canonical books can determine which books are God's Word and thus authoritative. These two principles have enabled God's people from the days of the Old and New Testaments to know which books made up God's Word. This explains why certain books were collected into what is called the Old Testament and certain books formed the New Testament. This also demonstrates that it was God and not humans who determined the canonicity of the biblical books. God's people simply recognized the books as coming from the hand of an accredited messenger of God. The continued use by the church of these books—and only these books—from the time of the apostles on has simply recognized what God had already signified and that is, that the books which constitute our Bible are the very Word of God.

In these caves at Qumran, near the Dead Sea, were found early copies of many Old Testament books.

A distinction needs to be made, however, between *canonicity* and *collection* of the biblical books. While no person or church

can make or pronounce a book to be canonical, yet it was the responsibility of the people to collect these canonical books and preserve them. Such collecting took place for both the Old and New Testaments. The Old Testament seems to have been collected by the days of Ezra and the "Great Synagogue," according to some scholars. By the time of Christ, it appears evident that the thirty-nine books of the Old Testament in the English Old Testament today were already collected and certainly were canonical. And the twenty-seven books of the English New Testament were collected by the time of the Council of Carthage (A.D. 397).

6. In its ability to satisfy the needs of humanity universally

Wherever the Bible has gone and in whatever nation, culture, or people its message has been given, people have sensed the answer to their deepest needs. And today the Bible's circulation in a multitude of translations has been worldwide. This makes a portion of the Bible available to 97 percent of the world's population. In addition, the whole Bible has been translated into more than 240 languages and the complete New Testament into over 320 languages.

Surely the Bible is unique in meeting human needs and its message transcends boundaries, cultures, difficult barriers, and varying conditions as it speaks to the human heart. It can truly be affirmed, "The Word of God is not bound."

The Old Testament

Foundational to Christianity, Islam, and Judaism is the Old Testament. The Jews, according to Paul, believed the Old Testament to be "the oracles of God" (Romans 3:2). For the Christian believer the character of the Old Testament is settled forever as the divinely inspired Word of God given under the infallible control of the Holy Spirit (Galatians 3:8; 2 Peter 1:20–21). This is so because Christ—the central figure of the Old Testament—put his seal upon the Old Testament, which, in his day, as in ours, contained the same books from Genesis to Malachi, though the order of the books was different (Luke 24:44ff.).

In our Bibles there are thirty-nine books arranged as follows:
17 historical books: Genesis–Esther
5 poetical books: Job–Song of Solomon
17 prophetic books: Isaiah–Malachi

The Hebrew Bible in contrast numbers these same books as twenty-four. The classification is three-fold:
The Torah or Law (5 books): Genesis–Deuteronomy
The Prophets or *Nebiim* (8 books): Joshua, Judges, Samuel, Kings, Isaiah, Jeremiah, Ezekiel, and the 12 Minor Prophets.
The Writings or *Kethubim* (11 books): Psalms, Proverbs, Song of Solomon, Ruth, Lamentations, Ecclesiastes, Esther, Daniel, Ezra–Nehemiah, and Chronicles.
　The idea of combining certain books in the Hebrew Bible was common. In the Hebrew canon 1 and 2 Samuel were counted as one, as were 1 and 2 Kings and 1 and 2 Chronicles. All twelve of the Minor Prophets were combined into one book—the reason for this was that they were so small (hence "Minor") that they did not want to risk losing any.
　This number of twenty-four books was further reduced to twenty-two by Josephus, a first-century historian, to make the books of the Old Testament correspond to the number of letters in the Hebrew alphabet. He accomplished this by attaching Ruth to Judges and Lamentations to Jeremiah.

The message of the Old Testament, regardless of the number and order of its books, is clear and the number of its books is identical with the King James Version today.

The central figure of the Old Testament, like that of the New, is the Messiah—Christ. Anticipated by the prophetic promises and represented symbolically in the sacrificial offerings, this Messiah would come to bring deliverance to his people. The very first redemptive promise indicated such deliverance: ". . . [The Messiah] shall bruise [the serpent's head]" (Genesis 3:15). From that promise on, through historical events, types, sacrificial offerings, judgments, and deliverances, God's people would learn much about this One who was to come. Thus the Old Testament story unfolds. It is a story of redemption—the story of a people who are to be holy unto their God. The object of God's sovereign purpose in saving us was to have a society of redeemed people.

To accomplish this purpose, God began with his initial promise in Genesis 3:15. This was a promise of hope to Adam and Eve, whose relationship to God had been broken by their sin. But the pursuit of sin continued in human history until the wickedness became so great that God had to destroy humankind in a flood—preserving only Noah and his family (Genesis 7:1).

With Noah began God's covenantal relationship, by which unilaterally he promised never to destroy humankind again by a great flood and sealed this covenant by the symbol of a rainbow.

With the inauguration of the covenant relationship there came about a special and significant way by which God deals with human beings. And the most important covenant for all humankind was now made. This was the Abrahamic Covenant (Genesis 12:1–3; 15:17–18; 17:1–2), which emphasized salvation by grace through the coming of One by whom all nations would be blessed. All of God's subsequent dealings redemptively would flow from this covenant and would come through the life and history of one nation—Israel.

God gave to this nation an affirmation that would set it apart from all other nations and would constitute its signal witness: "Hear, O Israel: The LORD our God is one LORD" (Deuteronomy 6:4). This monotheistic proclamation was strongly implanted in the heart of every Israelite and today is the unifying factor in the heart of every Jew.

Such an assertion did not prevent Christ from pronouncing that he is the incarnation and full revelation of that one God (John 10:29–38; 14:8–11; 17:21–22). Rather, Christ noted that because of this, "salvation is of the Jews" (John 4:22).

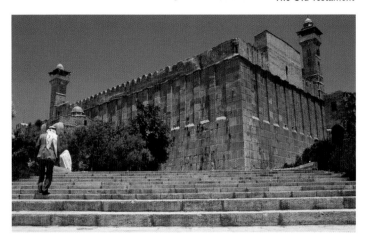

The story of God's dealings with the nation Israel is the story of the Old Testament, a story whose climax was to be this coming of God manifest in human flesh (John 1:14–18). Thus in the Old Testament there are the divine dealings with Israel that prepared the world for that moment when the fullness of time was come, and God would send forth his Son, made of a woman, made under the law (Galatians 4:4). Thus the Old Testament emphasizes God's preparation for the Incarnation.

The ancient Cave of Machpelah, Hebron, by tradition the burial place of Abraham and his family.

The outline of the history of the Old Testament can be helpful in understanding this preparation:

1. Primal History: The story of origins in Genesis 1–11: The creation to the scattering of the nations.

2. Patriarchal History: The story of Israel's founding fathers in Genesis 12–50: The call of Abraham to Joseph's demise.

3. Mosaic History: The story of Israel's wilderness wanderings in Exodus–Deuteronomy: Deliverance from Egypt to the death of Moses.

4. National History: The story of Israel and the promised land in Joshua–Malachi: The conquest of Canaan to the exile and restoration.

The book of Malachi closes the Old Testament; the voice of God in divine revelation is silent. Israel awaits the advent of her Messiah—even Christ.

Hebron.

The Pentateuch

The name by which the first five books of the Bible—Genesis, Exodus, Leviticus, Numbers, and Deuteronomy—are generally known is the Pentateuch. This word, composed of two Greek words *penta* (five) and *teuchos* (tool/volume) means five volume books, thus the five-fold manifestation of God's message to his people through Moses.

The Pentateuch has been the centre of controversy, especially in an organized sense since the seventeenth century because it reveals the origin of the universe and humanity. The controversy has centred on many focal points, but the authorship of the books is the most important because authorship and authenticity go together.

The attack upon the Pentateuch intensified in the late nineteenth and early twentieth centuries when it was generally agreed among critical scholars that Moses could not have written these books. The theory proposed in the place of Mosaic authorship was called the Documentary Theory. Analyzing the Pentateuch on the basis of the divine names and the codes of law, they came up with four basic documents: J, E, D, and P. The dates given to these documents were: J between 950–850 B.C.; E about 750 B.C.; D about 600 B.C., and P around 500 B.C. These letters stand for:

1. Two divine names with each name being more prominent in that particular document: in the J document, the name Jehovah was dominant, and in the E, the name Elohim.

2. The codes of the law, with D representing the Deuteronomist and P the priestly codes.

About 430 B.C. these four documents were combined into one document called the Pentateuch.

Today the Documentary Theory has been so refined by critical scholars that it is difficult to discuss the modern view without going into great detail. As someone has noted, the present state of the literary criticism of the Pentateuch is chaotic.

When one asserts that Moses was the author of the Pentateuch, it does not mean that he wrote every word. But it does mean that God revealed to him, under the control and guidance of the Holy Spirit, that which he wanted recorded. So, Moses, under this guidance and control, could have used various sources such

as oral transmission and some written records as God directed him. Certainly God would have had to reveal to Moses directly the creation narrative, and also God gave the ten commandments directly to Moses. Other events, of course, would be known to Moses because he was the leader of the Israelites in the wilderness wanderings. Perhaps he had the aid of scribes to record these events. That there were written records in Moses' day is seen from Numbers 21:14: "Wherefore it is said in the book of the wars of the LORD, What he did in the Red sea and in the brooks of Arnon." One portion that in all probability Moses did not write, unless he did it prophetically, was the account of his death (Deuteronomy 34). In conclusion, Moses as the author of the Pentateuch means that under the influence, guidance, and control of the Holy Spirit, the words in these books are the words of God in the literary style and personality of Moses.

St Catherine's Monastery, Sinai, near the mountain believed to be where Moses received the ten commandments.

To assert that Moses was the author of the Pentateuch does not necessarily prove that he was. Are there substantial reasons to undergird this assertion?

The last book of the Pentateuch which would inferentially include all the five books—the book of Deuteronomy—states that Moses wrote the Law: "And Moses wrote this law, and delivered it unto the priests the sons of Levi, which bare the ark of the covenant of the LORD, and unto all the elders of Israel" (Deuteronomy 31:9 with verses 24–26). Another statement in Exodus 34:27: "And the LORD said unto Moses, Write thou these words: for after the tenor of these words I have made a covenant

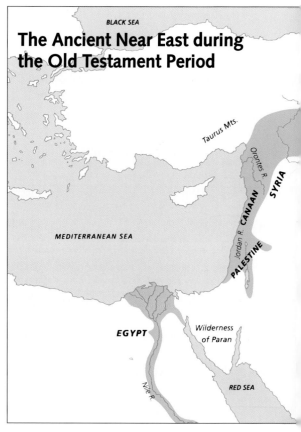

The Ancient Near East during the Old Testament Period

BLACK SEA

Taurus Mts.

Orontes R.

SYRIA

CANAAN

Jordan R.

PALESTINE

MEDITERRANEAN SEA

EGYPT

Wilderness of Paran

Nile R.

RED SEA

with thee and with Israel" (compare Leviticus 1:1; 4:1; 6:1; Numbers 1:1; 2:1; 4:1).

Other portions of the Old Testament testify to Moses' authorship: "And the children of the Levites bear the ark of God upon their shoulders with the staves thereon, as Moses commanded according to the word of the LORD" (1 Chronicles 15:15). And also in 2 Kings 18:12: "Because they obeyed not the voice of the LORD their God, but transgressed his covenant, and all that Moses the servant of the LORD commanded, and would not hear them, nor do them."

The prophets also join this testimony. The pre-exilic prophet Isaiah in Isaiah 1:10, writing about the immorality of God's peo-

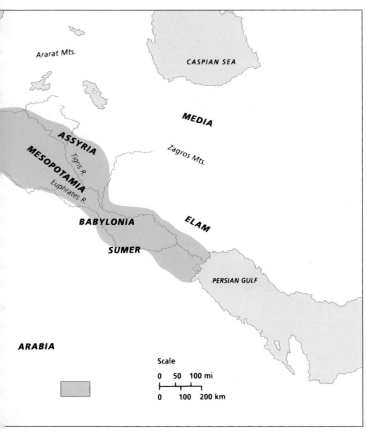

Ararat Mts.

CASPIAN SEA

MEDIA

ASSYRIA

Tigris R.

Zagros Mts.

MESOPOTAMIA

Euphrates R.

BABYLONIA

ELAM

SUMER

PERSIAN GULF

ARABIA

Scale

0   50   100 mi

0   100   200 km

ple in his day, notes the wickedness of Sodom and Gomorrah and speaks of the need to heed God's law. This notation is probably from Deuteronomy 32:32, which has already been declared as given by Moses. The post-exilic prophet Malachi writes: "Remember ye the law of Moses my servant, which I commanded unto him in Horeb for all Israel, with the statutes and judgments" (Malachi 4:4). Also Nehemiah 1:7 states this same conviction: "We have dealt very corruptly against thee, and have not kept the commandments, nor the statutes, nor the judgments, which thou commandest thy servant Moses." Such statements certainly indicate strongly that the Torah, or Law of God, as the Pentateuch was called by the Old Testament writers, had Moses as its author.

The Lord Jesus Christ set his seal of approval upon the Mosaic authorship of the Pentateuch. "And as touching the dead, that they rise: have ye not read in the book of Moses, how in the bush God spake unto him, saying . . ." (Mark 12:26). Then also: "And Jesus saith unto him, See thou tell no man; but go thy way, show thyself to the priest, and offer the gift that Moses commanded, for a testimony unto them" (Matthew 8:4; see also 19:7; Luke 16:29; 24:44; John 5:46,47). The final word for the believer regarding the authorship of the Pentateuch is Christ, and he has, in the verses noted, spoken unequivocally for the Mosaic authorship.

Additionally, the apostolic witness is just as strong. James, the leader of the Council at Jerusalem, stated: "For Moses of old time hath in every city them that preach him, being read in the synagogues every sabbath day" (Acts 15:21). Paul, when speaking about the blindness of the Jews, laments: "But even unto this day, when Moses is read, the veil is upon their heart" (2 Corinthians 3:15). The early church's endorsement of the Mosaic authorship of the Pentateuch is quite evident from these two powerful and influential apostles.

Combined with the above witnesses has been the almost universal view of both the Jews and the Christian church, until the nineteenth century, that Moses wrote the Pentateuch. The Samaritan Pentateuch, which dates from about 500 B.C., testifies to the authorship by Moses. The Apocrypha, written between our Old and New Testaments, also validates the Mosaic authorship: "While she was yet speaking these words, the young man said, Whom wait ye for? I will not obey the King's commandment; but I will obey the commandment of the law which was given unto our fathers by Moses" (2 Maccabees 7:30).

This evidence of the Mosaic authorship of the Pentateuch would seem to be so strong that no one could doubt that Moses was the author. But along with the denial of his authorship, the early advocates of the Documentary Theory made a number of other assertions that he could not have written it:

a. Writing was not invented at the time of Moses; yet the discovery of the Hammurabi's Code of Laws (dated about eighteenth century B.C.) exploded this view.

b. Names such as Abraham could not be individuals but signified tribes; yet the Mari tablets show that such personal names, even names of places similar to the biblical names, existed in patriarchal times.

c. Aramaic words were a sign of late dating, but the Ras Shamra tablets already contain Aramaic words showing this to be untrue.

The wind-eroded Sphinx near Cairo, Egypt. Tradition says that Moses was educated at Heliopolis.

d. Denial of the existence of the Hittites (who previously had been known from the Bible only) was contradicted by various documents of the ancient Near East.

Instances where archaeology sheds light on the customs of the ancient Near East which are seen in the biblical text could be multiplied. And such discoveries caution us not to be too hasty to deny the historical accuracy of such biblical books as those of the Pentateuch. Certainly no one should deny that Moses could have written the Pentateuch. As argument after argument against his authorship was advanced in the past, time has vindicated Moses and the Pentateuch.

This has not been accidental, for God is the sovereign God of history and, in giving his divine revelation in history, selected and prepared men to be the instruments for recording this revelation. Moses was such an instrument and, by background and learning, as the Scriptures declare, "was learned in all the wisdom of the Egyptians . . ." (Acts 7:22). This learning was very formidable in its breadth and scope. Tradition says that he was educated at Heliopolis. The curriculum was comprehensive and

23

would have included writing (see for instance the pictorial symbols of Egyptian); arithmetic (the Egyptians invented the numerals which we term Arabic and use today); the rudiments of geometry and trigonometry (witness the Pyramids); music (Moses would have a knowledge of music both vocal and instrumental, of harmony and rhythm [see for example Exodus 15:1, 20–21; Deuteronomy 32] and notice that the ancient tombs near the Pyramids reveal through drawings musicians who sang and played instruments); astronomy (Egyptian astronomers were able to determine with remarkable accuracy that the solar year had 364.25 days, that the sun was the centre of our universe, that the days and nights were caused by the revolution of the earth upon its axis, and that the moon received its light by reflection from the sun); law (administered by well-qualified judges, the Egyptians had a large body of laws); and science (Egyptians had rigid sanitation laws, an excellent knowledge of anatomy, allowed the practice of dissection of the human body, and were ably qualified in medicine and its application).

To be the author, therefore, of these books which would deal with such questions as the origin of the universe, the laws of religious sanitation, and a faith that would bring hope and deliverance to the world was certainly not beyond Moses' educational and religious preparation. For a revelation that would deal with such, Moses was selected and carefully prepared by God.

This divine revelation, contained in the Pentateuch, can be analyzed simply into three eras:

1. *Pre-history—the time of origins—Genesis 1–11*

Here is detailed the direct creation of the universe, the direct creation of humankind, the original sin of man, the story of Cain and Abel, the record of the generations of Adam, the universal flood, and the scattering of the nations descended from Noah.

2. *Patriarchal History—the origin of Israel—Genesis 12–50*

The call of Abraham and the story of God's covenantal relationship with him, the birth of Isaac (the son of promise), the selling of Joseph into Egypt, and the journey of Jacob and his sons to Egypt during the great famine which resulted in the salvation of the nation of Israel as God providentially rescued them through Joseph.

3. *Providential Deliverance of Israel from Egypt—the origin of the Law—Exodus to Deuteronomy*

Dealing with the redemption of the children of Israel from bondage in Egypt, their wanderings in the wilderness after the inauguration of the Passover, the giving of God's providential

guidance with cloud by day and the pillar of fire by night, the declaration of the Law, the building of the tabernacle, the origin of the priesthood and offerings, the numberings of the tribes of Israel, and the detailed review of the Law.

The Pentateuch closes with God's giving Moses a view of the promised land, followed by God's taking him in death—his death resulting from his disobedience to God in *striking* the rock rather than *speaking* to it, an act which cost him entrance into Canaan but not into heaven. The Pentateuch reveals the origin and continuation of God's marvellous grace.

Doctrinally, the Pentateuch is the seed-plot of the Bible: it teaches creation—the only satisfactory and realistic explanation of the universe's origin; it teaches the origin of sin—why humans act as they do and need salvation; it teaches salvation by grace and demonstrates that there can be no other way—we cannot save ourselves, whether by obedience to the law or any human merit; and it teaches the hope of eternal life. Without these Pentateuchal teachings, there would be no hope for humankind. The rest of the Bible enlarges on these themes and guarantees the reality and availability of hope and salvation to humankind.

A nomadic settlement in the Sinai desert. The children of Israel lived as wilderness nomads after the Exodus.

Genesis

Genesis has given to our language a word which refers to beginning or commencement, and because of its early chapters relates to origins: that of the universe, humankind, sin, salvation and many others. The word comes from the title given to the book in the Greek translation of the Old Testament. The English transliteration of the Greek is "genesis." In the Hebrew text, *Bereshith* has the same idea of origins and is translated "in the beginning."

Genesis opens with one of the most majestic statements in all of literature: "In the beginning God . . ." This sets the stage for everything that is to follow. It points to the sovereign rulership of God and demonstrates that all that happens in history will really be his story. His providential control will guide all history to its intended goal and consummation. Genesis cannot be read and studied without realizing that God is on the throne and his end will be achieved.

There are several unique features about Genesis:

1. It is doctrinally basic to all other books of the Bible dealing with the profound doctrines of God, creation, humankind, sin, judgment, mercy, origin of nations and their early history, salvation by grace through faith, angels, substitutionary sacrifice (Abraham and Isaac, Genesis 22), providence, and preservation by God as demonstrated in the lives of the patriarchs—especially Joseph.

2. It deals with a subject that has brought much conflict—the relationship of the Bible to science. Such a relationship has caused many harsh statements on both sides of the issue. Many scientists, as well as biblical scholars, have asserted that Genesis is not a textbook on science—and it is not! Others have said that the Bible deals with only the spiritual and eternal, while science deals only with the mundane and temporal. Each is a separate entity and one area must not invade the other. Careful scholarship on both sides, however, has realized that true science and true interpretation are not in conflict. Patience, understanding, and dedication to the truth of the Bible will ultimately bring that light which illumines both God's Word and God's world. For no clearer statement can be made concerning the universe's origin than: "In the beginning God created the heaven and the earth" (Genesis 1:1) and on the origin of man: "So God created man in his own image . . ." (Genesis 1:27).

3. It declares the deep reality of complete obedience and faith

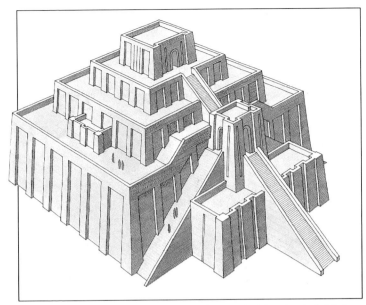

An artist's reconstruction of a Mesopotamian ziggurat. The Tower of Babel may have looked similar.

in God. Faith thus will never have a proper definition without a reference to Abraham and his implicit commitment to God (compare Genesis chapters 12; 15; 17; 21–22 with Romans 4 and 5; Galatians 3; Hebrews 11). It is that faith which justifies and declares a man righteous—without works.

STUDY GUIDE OUTLINE TO GENESIS

1. The Creation of the Universe and Man *1:1–2:25*
2. The Commencement of Human Sin *3:1–5:32*
3. The Condemnation of Humankind *6:1–8:22*
4. The Covenant with Noah *9:1–29*
5. The Course of the Nations *10:1–11:32*
6. The Call and Covenant of Abraham *12:1–17:27*
7. The Consuming of Sodom and Gomorrah *18:1–20:38*
8. The Confirmation of Abraham's Covenant with Isaac *21:1–26:35*
9. The Craftiness of Jacob *27:1–36:43*
10. The Consecrated Life of Joseph *37:2–50:25*

Exodus

One of the greatest events in the history of God's people was their departure from the land of Egypt, where they had been in bondage and slavery for some four hundred years. This book, describing this great event and subsequent developments before reaching the promised land, is called Exodus from the Greek word given in the Septuagint, or Greek translation of the Old Testament. The meaning of the word is "departure," "going out," or "exit."

Since the book records the events associated with the departure from Egypt, two issues confront the reader: When did this event occur, and who was this obstinate, cruel, and hard-hearted Pharaoh who broke his word to Moses so frequently?

Though the date of the Exodus has been hotly disputed, conservative scholars relying upon the statement of 1 Kings 6:1 ("And it came to pass in the four hundred and eightieth year after the children of Israel were come out of the land of Egypt, in the fourth year of Solomon's reign over Israel . . .") believe that by taking the date of the beginning of Solomon's reign (about 971 B.C.) and deducting the four years which elapsed before he started to build the temple, the date 967 B.C. is ascertained. Adding the 480 years noted above, the date for the Exodus is 1447 B.C. With the forty years of wandering in the wilderness, the time of entrance into the land of Canaan would be about 1407 B.C. According to the archaeologist Garstang, the

Fertile land on the banks of the Nile River, Egypt. One of the greatest events in the history of God's people was their departure from the land of Egypt.

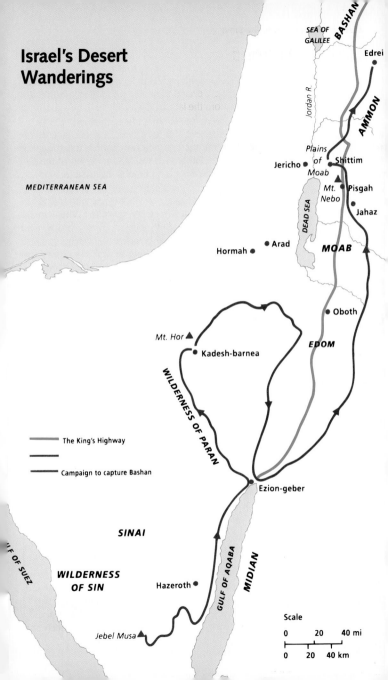

Israel's Desert Wanderings

MEDITERRANEAN SEA

SEA OF GALILEE

BASHAN

Edrei

Jordan R.

AMMON

Plains of Moab

Jericho ● ● Shittim

Pisgah

Mt. Nebo

Jahaz

DEAD SEA

MOAB

Hormah ● ● Arad

Oboth ●

Mt. Hor ▲

● Kadesh-barnea

EDOM

WILDERNESS OF PARAN

The King's Highway

Campaign to capture Bashan

Ezion-geber

SINAI

WILDERNESS OF SIN

GULF OF AQABA

MIDIAN

Hazeroth ●

Jebel Musa ▲

ULF OF SUEZ

Scale

0   20   40 mi

0   20   40 km

Tel-el-Amarna Letters date the fall of Jericho around 1400 B.C. And these same letters describe a people called "Habiru" who had invaded Palestine and were capturing the land. Many scholars identify these people as Hebrews at the time of Joshua's conquest.

If this is the date for the Exodus, and solid evidence from archaeology and from the biblical record of the events (notably the statement of 1 Kings 6:1) indicates that this is the date for the Exodus, then the Pharaoh of this Exodus was Amenhotep II. His reign stretched over the years from about 1436 to 1415 B.C. and he was the one who hardened his heart against Moses and the Israelites and whose word could not be trusted until God had to deal very severely with him by taking his first born in death (Exodus 12:29).

From these circumstances comes the theme of Exodus, which is redemption or deliverance. Bringing Israel into a very special relationship to himself through the Abrahamic Covenant, God now deals with them on a redemptive basis through which he will graphically and dramatically work out his eternal plan of salvation for humankind.

Unique Features of Exodus

1. The use of miracles to accredit God's messenger so as to accomplish God's purpose in delivering God's people from slavery and sustain them in their wanderings as they made their way to the promised land. This lesson in God's supernatural power forms a basis for the believer's confidence in his or her daily walk in this life.

2. The institution of the Passover as both a means which brought about the release of Israel from physical slavery and the believer from the penalty of spiritual sin. This drama of the shedding of the blood of a lamb forms the typical analogy of the only way of salvation through the shedding of the blood of God's Lamb (John 1:29 with Exodus 12:1–36).

3. The providential provision of God as he supplies the needs of his people in the material as well as the spiritual needs of their daily experiences: the manna (Exodus 16:35; John 6:30–35; 1 Corinthians 10:3); the rock (Exodus 17:6; John 6:35; 1 Corinthians 10:4).

4. The presence of God with his people as he guides them day by day and protects them by night. This symbolizes that God is always with his people to guide, control, and protect them in every circumstance: the cloud by day and the pillar of fire by night (Exodus 13:21–22 with Matthew 28:20); the tabernacle

with its shekinah glory and the mercy seat, all showing God's presence (Exodus 40:38–40; John 1:14–18; 21:3); and God's place of reconciliation and propitiation—the mercy seat (Romans 3:25; 1 John 2:2; 4:10 with Exodus 37:6–9).

The barren wasteland of the Sinai desert. God sustained his people in their wanderings as they made their way to the promised land.

5. The inauguration of the principle of mediatorship through the priesthood, which points up also the mediating ministry of the Saviour (Exodus 28:1–29:9; 1 Timothy 2:5–6).

6. The convicting work of the divine law upon the sinner as exhibited in the Ten Commandments given in the Mosaic Covenant and the relationship of law to grace as seen in Galatians (Exodus 20:1–26; Galatians 3:1; 4:19–31; Romans 4:1–25).

Through these unique features the redemptive theme of Exodus is worked out and emphasizes anew that which was strikingly revealed, that even in the giving of the law and in the construction of the altar (the place of sacrificial offerings) no tool (the obvious sign of human merit) should touch it: "For by grace are ye saved through faith; and that not of yourselves: it is the gift of God: Not of works, lest any man should boast" (Ephesians 2:8–9).

STUDY GUIDE OUTLINE TO EXODUS

1. The Cruelty under the Pharaohs *1:1–2:25*
2. The Call of Moses, the Deliverer *3:1–4:31*
3. The Contest with Pharaoh *5:1–13:19*
4. The Care of God Providentially over Israel *13:20–19:2*
5. The Covenant with Moses for Israel *19:3–24:8*
6. The Construction and Use of the Tabernacle for Worship *24:9–30:38*

Leviticus

Aaron, the brother of Moses, was ordained of God to be a priest. His sons and descendants would occupy the priestly position in Israel. The rest of his tribe, that of Levi, would be assistants to this Aaronic priesthood. The title "Leviticus," meaning "pertaining to Levites," comes from the Latin translation of the Old Testament—the Vulgate. From the opening word of the Hebrew text come the words "and he called" by which the Jews called it, and in the Talmudic times it was called "Law of the Priests."

The theme of the book is the separation and sanctification of the chosen people unto God, who is infinitely holy. This theme centres on the oft repeated: "For I am the LORD your God: ye shall therefore sanctify yourselves, and ye shall be holy; for I am holy . . ." (Leviticus 11:44, compare verse 45; 19:2; 20:7, 26). To attain this holiness, however, entrance into God's presence comes only through the sacrificial offering: "For the life of the flesh is in the blood: and I have given it to you upon the altar to make an atonement for your souls: for it is the blood that maketh an atonement for the soul" (Leviticus 17:11). Sacrificial offerings have the two-fold purpose of expiation—the blotting out of sin—and consecration—the divine act of separation unto God.

Since Leviticus deals with the priesthood—mediators between God and man—and the sanctification of God's people, then it is necessary that God lay down regulations governing the total life of his people. Such regulations, of course, flow out of the "covenant relationship between God and his people." Consequently, there is not only the need for expiation of sin, but there need to be laws which deal with religious conduct, ethical purity, and civic responsibility. This highlights not only the love of the Israelite for God, but also his love for his neighbour (Leviticus 19:18). The law can now be summed up in such a two-fold love (Mark 12:30–31).

The outstanding feature of Leviticus, as it relates to sacrifice, is the Day of Atonement. Stringent requirements governed the observance of this annual occurrence. No one could come into God's presence in the holy place except the high priest, and he could only because of the blood.

The imagery of this Day of Atonement provides the basis for an understanding of the book of Hebrews, which presents Christ as the great High Priest and the superiority of his priesthood—after the order of Melchizedek—over that of Aaron. In this imagery, and the elements associated with it in the sacrificial offerings,

The Tabernacle

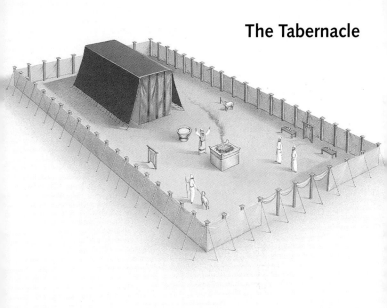

a number of factors are revealed:

1. Substitution—the whole picture here and in Hebrews is that of the offering taking the place of the offerer.

2. Vindication—the holiness of God and the revelation of that holiness as seen in his law (Leviticus 16:9; Romans 3:24–26) is vindicated. This is seen in the slain goat which is offered by the high priest.

3. Propitiation—here God's righteousness is satisfied and here "at the mercy-seat" God withholds judgments and displays mercy.

4. Remission—signified by the live goat as it is sent away into the wilderness. The sins of the offerer are forgiven, or remitted, or sent away, and life is renewed (Leviticus 4:35; 16:21; Matthew 26:28).

5. Perfection—in the offering because there must be no blemish (Leviticus 1:3–9) in the animal. Corresponding to this, Christ is the sinless offering (Hebrews 4:15).

6. Communion—the privileged fellowship of the believer with God is pictured in the peace offering which symbolizes peace with God and the fellowship of communication (Leviticus 3:1–17; Ephesians 2:14–18; Colossians 1:20).

STUDY GUIDE OUTLINE TO LEVITICUS

1. Instruction for the Sacrifices *1–7*
2. Consecration of the Aaronic Priesthood *8–10*
3. Legislation for Holy Living *11–15*
4. Inauguration of the Day of Atonement *16*
5. Application of Ethical Standards *17–22*
6. Convocations, Feasts, Seasons, and Sabbatical Years *23–25*
7. Conditions for Blessing, or Chastisement, for Disobedience *26*
8. Estimation of Vows *27*

Numbers

The rather ordinary title for the book of Numbers comes from both the Greek *arithmoi* and the Latin *numeri*, meaning "numbers." And this relates to the two numberings of Israel (chapters 1 and 26). In the Hebrew text, however, the name by which the Jews called the book comes from "*Bemidbar,*" which means "in the desert" or "in the wilderness."

This book encompasses the time from Israel's encampment at Mount Sinai and the preparations made for departure from that area, also including the wilderness wanderings to their arrival in the plains of Moab. All of this occupied almost thirty-nine years.

Opposition to the authenticity of the book has come from two basic charges—the objection to the Mosaic authorship and the hostility to the supernatural and miraculous care of a people who had grown to an incredible number from a small beginning. The assertion made is that it would be utterly impossible for the Israelites in such a short span of time in Egypt to grow from some seventy families to over 600,000 fighting men with women and children; the total amount of such persons would be between 2.5 and 3 million. How could such a number be fed for almost forty years?

The answer to the first charge is found in the defence noted above about the Mosaic authorship of the Pentateuch. It was shown there that there are no substantial reasons advanced against Moses' authorship that would overthrow the traditional view that he wrote all five books. The book of Numbers obviously forms a unity with the rest of the Pentateuchal books.

To the second charge, the book of Numbers gives its own

answer: the people were fed by the supernatural power of God, who had provided manna (11:6–9) and quails from the sea (11:31). As to the tremendous growth in numbers, the reason why they were oppressed in Israel, why God ultimately delivered them, and why they were in the wilderness was that the Egyptians feared them. They had grown so rapidly because of the unusual fertility of Israelite women (Exodus 1:7–22).

Some Important Spiritual Truths in Numbers

1. One of the most beautiful benedictions that God's representatives can bestow upon God's people is given in chapter 6:24–26. This is a prayer asking for God's protection, care, and blessing upon his people. If God's covenant with them is kept, then God's blessing will follow.

2. The need in times of decision relating to spiritual matters that the believer must "stand still, and I will hear what the LORD will command . . ." (Numbers 9:8). One needs to pause before God, be still and listen to what God has to say and then to obey him (Psalm 46:10).

3. The entire book of Numbers again and again stresses the need for implicit trust. This is especially true between those who are leaders of God's people—there must be a recognition of proper areas of command and responsibility. The seditious actions of Miriam and Aaron illustrate this (12:1–16).

4. A leader of God's people should always be characterized by genuine humility and meekness, especially when his or her leadership and actions are questioned (12:3).

5. Opportunity to do God's will must be seized when it presents itself. The spies visited the promised land, but only two had the courage to recommend that God's will be done. With God all things are possible (chapter 13).

6. Obedience to God is necessary, and though disobedience takes place, it does not mean that God does not bless. God's blessing, therefore, is not always the sign that God's servant is doing God's will in God's way. Moses was ordered to *speak* to the rock that water might flow, but Moses *struck* the rock in anger. Moses disobeyed but the blessing came; as a result Moses lost the privilege to lead God's people into the promised land (20:1–12).

7. Each individual had an assigned responsibility in the work in Israel for the nation's ongoing well-being. For the believer today, spiritual gifts are bestowed to enable him or her to take responsibility in the local church for its ongoing work (Numbers 1:1–10:10 with 1 Corinthians 12:1–31; Ephesians 4:11–13).

STUDY GUIDE OUTLINE TO NUMBERS

1. The Preparation for Departure from Sinai *1–14*
   a. Organization of the camp *1:1–4:49*
   b. Regulations for purity and separation *5:1–6:27*
   c. Separation for spiritual service *7:1–10:10*
   d. Provisions for marching *10:11–11:35*
   e. Dissatisfaction among various groups *12:1–14:45*

2. The Problems of the Wilderness Sojourn
   15:1–21:35
   a. Commandments to the people *15*
   b. Concepts of the priesthood *16:1–18:32*
   c. Consecration rituals *19:1–20:21*

3. The Prophecies of Balaam *22:1–25:18*
   a. The curse of Israel attempted *22:1–23:12*
   b. The conquest of Israel predicted *23:13–24:25*
   c. The compromise with Midian accomplished *25*

4. The Possession of the Land Anticipated *26–36*
   a. The census *26:1–65*
   b. The appointments *27:1–30:17*
   c. The attack on Midian *31:1–54*
   d. The instruction for the occupation *32–36*

8. A remarkable prophecy concerning the Messiah came from the lips of a pagan prophet under the control of God (24:17). But this same prophet caused a sin for money on the part of Israel that resulted in the death of 24,000 Israelites. What could not be accomplished by direct prophecy by a pagan prophet to curse Israel was accomplished indirectly by getting Israel to sin. Thus, in Scripture, Balaam's name is associated with that which is false and corrupt: the way of Balaam (2 Peter 2:15); the error of Balaam (Jude 11); the doctrine of Balaam (Revelation 2:14).

Deuteronomy

The meaning of Deuteronomy is "second lawgiving" or "repetition of the law." The word comes both from the Greek translation of the Old Testament (Septuagint) and the Latin translation (the Vulgate). The Greek word is *deuteronomion* and the Latin *deuteronomium.* The Hebrew name is *Elleh haddebarim,* the first words in the Hebrew text, and means "These are the words."

Deuteronomy contains the last addresses given by Moses to

God's people in the plains of Moab. These addresses are not simply a repetition of the law. They are really a distillation of that religious faith which is the content and ethical conduct demanded
of a people who are in covenant relationship with the true and
living God. The basis of this faith, and the demands placed upon
Israel, are found in two key statements in this book:

The sun is
reflected off the
surface of the
Dead Sea. On the
distant shore are
the Plains of
Moab.

1. "Hear, O Israel: The LORD our God is one LORD: And thou
shalt love the LORD thy God with all thine heart, and with all thy
soul, and with all thy might" (Deuteronomy 6:4–5).

2. "For thou art an holy people unto the LORD thy God: the
LORD thy God hath chosen thee to be a special people unto himself, above all people that are upon the face of the earth. The
LORD did not set his love upon you, nor choose you, because ye
were more in number than any people . . . but because the LORD
loved you, and because he would keep the oath which he had
sworn unto your fathers . . ." (Deuteronomy 7:6–8).

Here is the *source* of the covenant relationship between God
and his people: the *sovereign choice* of the only God of heaven
and earth; here also is the *ground*—or *basis*—on which this choice
was made: the gracious love of this God; and here is the *moti-
vation* by which their discharge of this covenant responsibility
will be governed: "thou shalt love the LORD thy God with all thine
heart."

Whether the people have been faithful to this covenant will
be judged by obedience or disobedience to the law by which
they will be immeasurably blessed; if unfaithful to this law, they
will be severely punished (Deuteronomy 29:9–29). But obedi-

MOAB

STUDY GUIDE OUTLINE TO DEUTERONOMY

1. The Conflict in the Wilderness Journeys Reviewed *1–4*
2. The Commandments of the Sinaitic Laws Restated *5–26*
3. The Commendations for Obedience and the Condemnation for Disobedience Uttered *27–28*
4. The Covenant Relating to the Land Detailed *29–30*
5. The Concluding Events Recited *31–34*

ence must always flow out of a loving heart. For obedience to the ritual of law can never take the place of obedience through the response of love (1 Samuel 15:22). To read this book is to feel the heartbeat of God as he seeks to find the pulse of our loving response and thus display a vital relationship of a covenant people. So Deuteronomy is not to be taken simply as a resumé of cold legislative demands by God upon his people but a compassionate loving desire of God for our dutiful response to be grounded in an incomparable loving compact.

Distinctive Teachings in Deuteronomy

1. God shows clearly that he will not always answer our prayers according to our desires. Moses pleaded anew for the privilege of entering the promised land, but God denied his request and reminded him of his disobedience through anger at the rebellion of God's people (3:23–28).

2. The most important commandment of God is to humankind and the most important responsibility of people in this life is to love God with all their being (6:5; 10:12; 11:1, 13, 22).

3. The choice made sovereignly by God concerning Israel as his people bears a specific relationship to God's command to that people. God expects devotion and obedience (chapter 11).

4. The believer must always be alert to any possible idolatry. An idol is anything that comes between an individual and his or her relationship to God (compare chapter 7).

5. God is faithful to his promises to his people. God's blessings flow not from our righteousness but God's grace. Rebellion, however, will bring God's punishment (compare chapters 9–10).

6. The great prophecy of a prophet "like unto Moses" found its fulfilment in Christ (John 5:46; Acts 3:22). Deuteronomy reinforces the great role of God's people as the channels through which salvation would come to mankind (John 4:22).

7. The graciousness of God in providing refuge for his people in time of need is seen in the choice of cities of refuge (4:41–43). The plan for their use is seen in 19:1–13. For the believer, God

is a place of refuge and a very present help in time of trouble (Psalms 27:5; 91:1–11).

8. God is the God of history, and he has painted the history of his people on the canvas of his Word. The history of the Jews has testified to this, and the Jew—who is the enigma of history—is also the great vindication of the truthfulness of God's Word (chapters 28–30).

9. The faithful reading and study of God's Word is necessary to keep us from sin and disobedience (31:1–13).

10. God's opportune call always comes at the right moment for a person prepared to respond to it. Such preparation comes many times in working with and in the shadow of another servant of God, as Joshua did in faithful relationship to Moses (31:7–8).

11. God, in his own providence and time, removes his workers for nobody is indispensable. Yet when that time comes, it is not always easy for the worker, as the sorrowful scene on Mount Nebo reveals (34:1–4).

12. Though God buries his workers, his work always goes on (34:5–12).

An orthodox Jew reads from the Hebrew Scriptures at Jerusalem's holy Western Wall. The faithful reading and study of God's Word is necessary to keep us from sin and disobedience.

The Historical Books

The books of Joshua through Esther have been called the historical books because they detail the historical events of Israel's history from the conquest of Canaan through the Assyrian and Babylonian captivities to the return and restoration under Ezra–Nehemiah. Though primarily detailing historical events, they cover chronologically the rest of the biblical material through the ministry of Malachi. Thus, they embrace a period of almost a thousand years.

Joshua secured the promised land for Israel; the judges sought to guard it from oppression until the time under Samuel when the people besought God for a king, as Moses had predicted they would (Deuteronomy 17:14). God then granted to them a king, Saul, "who stood head and shoulders above all Israel" and who, though beginning auspiciously, prostituted his position through disobedience, so that God took the kingdom from him (1 Samuel 15:1–35). In his place God anointed David, to whom he gave the promise that his kingdom would last forever (2 Samuel 7:16).

The kingdom of Israel from the removal of Saul until the time of David's actual ascent to the throne experienced much turmoil, as Saul sought to kill David, and David, not desiring to lift his hand against the Lord's anointed, fled before Saul. The picture of this time is one of a newly anointed king torn between his love for and loyalty to Saul and patiently awaiting the time and circumstances of God's appointment when he would occupy the throne.

Under David and Solomon, the kingdom reached a height of glory, power, and extent which it had never before attained. The apostasy of Solomon, however, ultimately brought about the division of the kingdom into the kingdom of Israel (the ten northern tribes), which continued until 722 B.C. when it was conquered by the Assyrians, and the kingdom of Judah (the two southern tribes), which were taken into captivity in Babylon in 586 B.C. when defeated by Nebuchadnezzar.

The historical books conclude with the return of God's people from captivity under Ezra and Nehemiah and their restoration in the land.

Joshua

The name of this book comes from the leader of the Israelites during the conquest of Canaan: Joshua. The book tells the story of Israel's entering the promised land under Joshua's leadership and settling in the land. Though the tribes of Reuben, Gad, and the half-tribe of Manasseh remained on the east side of the Jordan, the others crossed over and settled in their assigned places. The struggle which led to the settlement was not an easy one, and on several occasions supernatural intervention was necessary.

Joshua's name means "Jehovah saves" or "Jehovah is salvation." The Hebrew name Joshua corresponds to the Greek name Jesus. Thus, in the coming of the Lord Jesus and in his name "Jesus," there is an analogy between the Joshua of the Old Testament and the Jesus of the New. As Joshua was chosen and commissioned to go into Canaan to capture the land for God's people and was assured by God that he would be with him, so the believer is commissioned by the Lord Jesus to go forth preaching the gospel and is assured that the Lord Jesus will be with him (Matthew 28:19–20; Joshua 3:7). As Joshua led the Israelites into the promised land, so the Lord Jesus leads those who trust him into the promised heaven. As Joshua spent years in the shadows preparing under Moses' leadership to lead God's people (Exodus 17:8–16; 33:11; Numbers 33–34; Deuteronomy 31:7), so the Lord Jesus spent years in quiet preparation to give his life as a ransom for sinners (Matthew 20:28).

Many have objected to the authorship of this book being assigned to Joshua. They claim that the book is a composite work from a number of sources and later compiled by a number of editors. While Joshua no doubt used sources, he nevertheless wrote the book, apart from some obvious sections, such as the record of his death (24:29–30). Joshua refers, for instance, to the book of Jashan (10:13) as one of his sources. Evidence that he wrote much of the book comes from the fact that he claims to be an eye-witness (5:1). There is no adequate reason that can be advanced against Joshua's authorship. The Talmud also supports Joshua's authorship.

The purpose of the book is clearly to record the events associated with the settlement of Israel in the promised land. It forms, therefore, the historical connecting link between the preparatory stages of Israel's life, as recorded in the Pentateuch, and their settled national life in Canaan. It depicts the military struggle for Canaan and the dividing of the land among the tribes who

STUDY GUIDE OUTLINE TO JOSHUA
1. **The Conquest of Canaan** *1–12*
   a. The charges delivered *1: 1–2:24*
   b. The crossing effected *3:1–5:1*
   c. The camp at Gilgal described *5:2–15*
   d. The campaigns conducted *6–12*
2. **The Settlement of Canaan** *13–24*
   a. The assigned portions designated *13–21*
   b. The charges to the tribes delivered *22–23*
   c. The covenant renewed *24*

entered the land. In all of this the supernatural power of God in fulfilling his promises to his people is revealed.

Central Features of Joshua

1. God displays that he is the God of faithfulness and power. He keeps his covenant agreement (chapters 1–6).

2. God cannot tolerate sin and when it occurs, he lifts his hand and humankind suffers the consequences of sin (chapter 7); when sin is dealt with, God's leading and blessing are restored (chapter 8).

3. God reveals his power by special means and miracles when his people need him. The miracle of the long day illustrates this. The sun was ordered to stand still and it did so (10:12–14).

4. God's declaration that the Canaanites should be exterminated has been hard for some to comprehend, but when the immorality of the people is fully understood then we understand its necessity (Deuteronomy 7:1–5; Joshua 11:20). The Canaanites were snake worshippers and engaged in licentious fertility cult rituals with sexual orgies and vices. In this way they worshipped their gods. Perhaps this explains the occupation of Rahab. Was she a religious prostitute? God did not want his people to be contaminated by such practices or adopt them. When the Israelites did not fully exterminate them, they fell into their sinful practices again and suffered God's judgment and punishment in captivity. Again, disobedience brings its own punishment.

5. God commanded the people to erect a memorial of twelve stones taken from the Jordan following the crossing, in order that through it they might teach their children to know God's might, and reverence the Lord God forever (4:1–24). For the believer, this stresses the need for the instruction of children in God's Word and work that they might commit their life unto him.

6. God lays down to Israel, through Joshua, the need for everyone to make an eternal decision to choose or reject God (24:14–15). It is a decision that every person must make when so confronted.

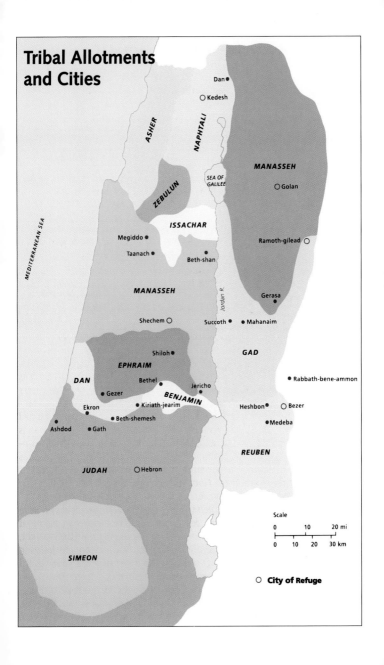

Tribal Allotments and Cities

Dan ●

○ Kedesh

ASHER

NAPHTALI

ZEBULUN

SEA OF GALILEE

MANASSEH

○ Golan

ISSACHAR

Megiddo ●

Ramoth-gilead ○

Taanach ●

Beth-shan ●

MEDITERRANEAN SEA

MANASSEH

Jordan R.

Gerasa ●

Shechem ○

Succoth ●   ● Mahanaim

Shiloh ●

GAD

EPHRAIM

DAN

Bethel ●

● Rabbath-bene-ammon

● Gezer

Jericho ●

BENJAMIN

Ekron ●

● Kiriath-jearim

Heshbon ●   ○ Bezer

● Beth-shemesh

Ashdod ●   ● Gath

● Medeba

REUBEN

JUDAH

○ Hebron

SIMEON

Scale

0   10   20 mi

0   10   20   30 km

○ **City of Refuge**

From Judges to the Divided Kingdom

Date	Biblical data	Judge
1367–1359	Judges 3:8	
1359–1319	Judges 3:11	Othniel
1319–1301	Judges 3:14	
1301–1221		Ehud, Shamgar
1221–1201	Judges 4:3	
1201–1161	Judges 5:31	Deborah and Barak
1161–1154	Judges 6:1	
1154–1110	Judges 8:28	Gideon, his sons
	Judges 9:22	Abimelech
	Judges 10:7f.	Tola, Jair
1110–1104	Judges 12:7	Jephthah
1104–1064	Judges 13:1	Ibzan, Elon, Adbon
	Judges 15:20, 16:31	Samson (c 1094–74)
	1 Samuel 4:18	Eli (40 yrs.; Septuagint =
1064–1044	1 Samuel 7:2	Samuel
1044–1004	Acts 13:21	Saul
1011–971	2 Samuel 5:5	David
971–931	1 Kings 11:42	Solomon
931	1 Kings 12:19	Division of the Kingdom

Judges

The story of Judges is the recital of the events relating to Israel's adjustment in the land, following its settlement by Joshua and the tribes that crossed the Jordan. It is a story of the tribes becoming political entities in themselves, seeking to settle the territories and get adequate territory to sustain themselves. Added to this was the spiritual infidelity that characterized God's people. Having failed to pursue relentlessly, God's command to exterminate the Canaanites utterly and their idolatrous worship, the Israelites fell easily into the trap of idolatrous compromise.

From the political circumstances when various peoples oppressed the Israelite tribes, God sent them leaders to rally them and, when they repented of their backsliding, gave them peri-

Oppressor/Rest	Egyptian Pharaoh
Aramaean/Mesopotamian oppression in days of Assur-ubailit	
REST	Horemhab (1342–14)
Moabites	
REST	Ramses II (1301–1234)
	Merenptah (1234–22)
Canaanites	Ramses III (1195–64)
REST	
Midianites	
Ammonites	
	Ramses, IV–XI (1164–1085)
	Weak 20th Dynasty
Philistines (I)	Divided 21st Dynasty (1085–950)
Philistines (II)	

ods of rest—politically and spiritually—under these designated judges.

It is from the leadership of these judges that the book derives its name. The Hebrews called this book *shopetim* which means "judges." Over a period of Israel's history from Joshua's death until the advent of Samuel's leadership, some fifteen judges were raised up by God to rescue, sometimes militarily, this people from the hands of hostile oppressors and their spiritual declension.

With the coming of the judges, God began to rule over his people indirectly. The direct relationship that he had with the patriarchs, Moses, and Joshua began to fade. This period of the judges forms a prelude to that time when there would be a monarchy. Fulfilling the prophecy of Moses, the people under Samuel would begin to demand a king (Deuteronomy 17:14–20; 1 Samuel 8:1–22). And God granted them one.

STUDY GUIDE OUTLINE TO JUDGES

1. The Character of the Times *1:1–3:7*
2. The Conflicts of the Nations with the Judges *3:8–16:31*
3. The Consequences of Apostasy *17–21*

The period of the judges is characterized as that time when "every man did that which was right in his own eyes" (Judges 21:25). This statement reveals the lack of unity among the tribes. With no central government, it was difficult to maintain order—hence the frequency of changes in leadership and the need for God to manifest his power to deliver, sometimes miraculously.

The question of the authorship of the book cannot be settled with certainty. Most scholars simply state that it is unknown, while some assert that Samuel could have compiled the history of these times.

Some Outstanding Features of Judges

1. The obvious failure of Israel to be faithful to their covenant obligations. It did not take long for them to compromise spiritually with their idolatrous surrounding neighbours.

2. The obvious fidelity of God to his covenant responsibilities, and his gracious forgiveness of Israel when they repented. He then delivered them from their oppressors and gave them rest.

3. The very beautiful Song of Deborah (5:1–31), ascribing adoration and praise to God for all his providential goodness.

4. The patience of God as he encouraged Gideon by giving him assurance, through the fleece, of his power to deliver his people miraculously.

5. The sad spectacle of Samson, the Nazarite, who prostituted his spiritual relationship to God and sold himself and his usefulness to God for the lust of a heathen woman. But again God was faithful and restored him in his dying moments.

6. The terrible sin of the tribe of Benjamin, the resultant slaughter, and the eventual reconciliation of the other tribes with the tribe of Benjamin.

Sin again is shown to bring its own punishment and also shows that when people sin, they damage not only themselves but the innocent.

Ruth

One of the most beautiful stories of love and loyalty is found in Ruth. It is a story centring around Ruth, the main individual in the events recorded, events which appear to have occurred during the early history of the book of Judges. Her name, Ruth, has no certain meaning, though four possible ones have been suggested: "sightly," "friendship," "companion," "refreshment."

Bethlehem
•

The historical setting of the book is the time of the early part of the book of Judges. The time of the writing, however, was that of David—a descendant of Boaz and Ruth (4:17–21). The author of the book is unknown.

A famine, according to the story, forced Elimelech and Naomi to migrate to Moab. There their two sons, Mahlon and Chilion, married two Moabite women, Ruth and Orpah. A triple tragedy then struck the family when, in the course of time, all three men died.

The poignant part of the story comes when Naomi decides to return to Judah. Bidding good-bye to her daughters-in-law, Naomi insists that she must return home and they must remain in Moab. She tells them that, even if it were physically possible for her to bear sons, they would not be able to wait until the time for them to reach maturity for marriage. Though Orpah decides to remain in Moab, nothing can shake the dedication and determination of Ruth to go with Naomi. She states: ". . . for whither thou goest, I will go; and where thou lodgest, I will lodge: thy people shall be my people, and thy God my God: Where thou diest, will I die, and there will I be buried; the LORD do so to me, and more also, if anything but death part thee and me" (1:16–17).

The return to Judah displays the providence of God at work. Ruth, gleaning in the fields at harvest time in order to help support herself and Naomi, meets Boaz. Boaz is related to Elimelech and seeks to exercise the right of kinsman-redeemer. He then finds the nearest of kin and learns he is unable to fulfil such a responsibility (3:1–8), and thus Boaz can now exercise that right. Marrying Ruth, he raises up a seed unto Elimelech and Mahlon and thus fulfils the law of levirate marriage (Deuteronomy 25:5–10). Through this act, Ruth the Moabitess—a Gentile—comes into the messianic genealogy as the great-grandmother of David.

STUDY GUIDE OUTLINE TO RUTH

1. The Return of Naomi and Ruth to Bethlehem *1*
2. The Reapers of Boaz and Ruth's Gleaning *2*
3. The Relationship of Kinsman-Redeemer Invoked *3*
4. The Redemption of Naomi's Property and Ruth's Marriage *4*

Interesting Highlights of Ruth

1. The depth of love, loyalty, and spiritual dedication on the part of Ruth is heartwarming. By her action, she does womanhood a great service and honour by her tremendous depth of spiritual perception: "And thy God, [shall be] my God." Forsaking the paganism of her god, she received salvation from the true God.

2. The beautiful teaching that the Messiah is not simply the Saviour of the Jews, but also of all peoples in the world, is underscored. Because of this remarkable story, the Gentiles have been brought into the Messianic line, and an unusual story of redemption it is, for Rahab (a former religious harlot spared by Joshua from death) was the mother of Boaz (see Matthew 1:5).

3. The ancient law regulating the redemption of property is exercised by Boaz. The old custom of sealing a bargain or deed by drawing off the shoe (4:7) shows that the events took place before the inauguration of the monarchy. The symbolism would seem to indicate that the possession of the shoe allowed the individual to have the right to set foot upon that land—thus to own it.

4. The grace of God seems very evident in Ruth's case, as she was allowed to have the right of kinsman-redeemer exercised on her behalf. No Moabite or Ammonite was to be allowed to enter into the congregation of the Lord as stipulated by Deuteronomy 23:3: "An Ammonite or Moabite shall not enter into the congregation of the LORD; even to their tenth generation shall they not enter into the congregation of the LORD for ever." Grace, instead of law, operates in Ruth's case.

5. The book, therefore, gives the background of David and his patrilineage (1 Samuel 16:1–13), and explains why David trusted his parents to reside under Moab's protection for a time (1 Samuel 22:3–4).

1 & 2 Samuel

Since 1 and 2 Samuel were treated as one in the Hebrew text, it is best to consider them together here. In the English text, as well as the modern Hebrew Bible, they are listed as separate books. The Greek translation of the Old Testament also considered them separately, and called them Books of the Kingdoms. Along with the two books of Kings, they form the Books of the Kingdoms.

The books of Samuel cover a period of more than a century, from Hannah's vow through the bulk of David's reign. The purpose of the books is to record the events associated with the establishment of the monarchy, the anointing and decline of Saul's kingship, and the anointing and the greater part of David's rulership.

There is a sense in which Samuel is the main figure in these books, though the books record largely the events associated with Saul and David as kings. Samuel's importance comes not so much from what he did as who he was. He was the last judge, who connected the period of the judges with the period of the monarchy. He was of priestly lineage and was both a priest and a prophet (1 Samuel 3:20; 11:15; Acts 3:24). He was the spiritual leader and the man who had the ear of God. He it was who anointed both Saul and David. Without the work of Samuel, under divine guidance and control, the events of these books could not have taken place. For this reason the books bear his name.

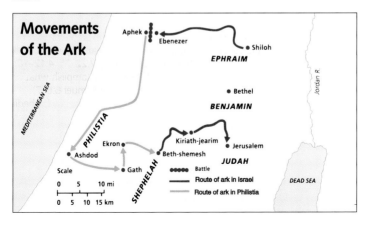

Movements of the Ark

Aphek • • • Ebenezer • Shiloh

EPHRAIM

MEDITERRANEAN SEA

PHILISTIA

• Bethel

BENJAMIN

Ekron • Kiriath-jearim
• Ashdod Beth-shemesh • Jerusalem
Scale • Gath *JUDAH*

Jordan R.

SHEPHELAH

•••• Battle
— Route of ark in Israel
— Route of ark in Philistia

DEAD SEA

0 5 10 mi
0 5 10 15 km

STUDY GUIDE OUTLINE TO 1 & 2 SAMUEL
1. The Appointment of Samuel to His Ministry
   1 Samuel 1–7
2. The Assent of God to Give Israel a King *1 Samuel 8*
3. The Anointing and Rule of Saul *1 Samuel 9–15*
4. The Antagonism of Saul towards David *1 Samuel
   16–31*
5. The Ascent of David to the Throne *2 Samuel 1–8*
6. The Activities of David as Ruler *2 Samuel 9–24*

The authorship of these books is uncertain. Certain names have been proposed as possible authors, and perhaps all of those suggested have had a part in the authorship. Men such as Samuel, Nathan, and Gad had written on occasion: "Then Samuel told the people the manner of the kingdom, and wrote it in a book, and laid it up before the LORD . . ." (1 Samuel 10:25). "Now the acts of David the king, first and last, behold, they are written in the book of Samuel the seer, and in the book of Nathan the prophet, and in the book of Gad the seer" (1 Chronicles 29:29). Perhaps Samuel wrote the early part of 1 Samuel, for his death is not recorded until 1 Samuel 25:1. The remainder of these books have no certain authors.

Though these books appear to be merely historical records, they have many spiritual lessons:

1. A mother so fully dedicated to God as Hannah set a high standard of dedication for believing mothers to imitate as they seek to rear their children for the Lord (1 Samuel 1:11, 24–28).

2. The need for a father to set the right example for his children and to discipline them correctly so that they might walk in God's way is illustrated in the failure of Eli (2:22–25; 4:12–18).

3. God is able, without man's help, to accomplish what he needs to do when occasion demands it (2 Samuel 6:6–7).

4. When God gives great responsibility, he demands obedience fully, and holds a man accountable when he disobeys (1 Samuel 12:8–14; 15:24–31).

5. One man, fully dedicated to and doing God's work in God's way, need fear no task set before him, no matter how seemingly impossible (1 Samuel 17:29–58).

6. There is always a divine order of authority and no person has the right to violate it. David's actions toward King Saul clearly establish this (1 Samuel 24:10; 26:33).

7. God has no additional word from beyond the grave for us, apart from what has already been revealed in his Word (1 Samuel 28:15–20; compare Luke 16:19–31).

8. It takes a great man to remember and provide for those who have no claim upon him when he reaches places of great responsibility and fame (2 Samuel 9:9–13).

9. When confronted by the conviction for our sin we should seek divine forgiveness, though we may have to suffer severely for our sin (2 Samuel 12:1–23).

10. A father's greatest suffering and sorrow sometimes comes from one of his own children (2 Samuel 15:7–12).

11. God never forgets his covenant promises to his people and makes a covenant with David that his kingdom will last forever (2 Samuel 7:4–17).

1 & 2 Kings

The English title for 1 and 2 Kings comes from Jerome's Vulgate, a Latin translation of the Old Testament. In the Hebrew text the books are a continuation of the history of the monarchy and form one book. The division into two books came with the Greek translation of the Old Testament, the Septuagint, where they were named 3 and 4 Kingdoms.

The author of the books, who cannot be identified with certainty, opens with the elevation to the throne of Solomon, and

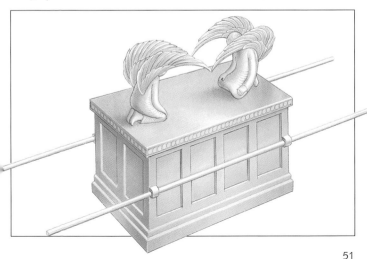

Northern Kingdom		Southern Kingdom	
First Dynasty			
Jeroboam I	931–910	Rehoboam	931–914
Nadab	910–909	Abijah	913–910
Second Dynasty			
Baasha	909–886	Asa	909–868
Elah	886–885		
(Zimri)	885		
Third Dynasty			
Omri	885–874		
Ahab	874–853	*Jehoshaphat	872–847
Ahaziah	853–852	*Jehoram	852–841
Joram	852–841	Ahaziah	841
		Athaliah	841–835
Fourth Dynasty			
Jehu	841–814	Joash	835–796
Jehoahaz	814–798		
*Jehoash	798–782	*Amaziah	796–767
*Jeroboam II	793–753	*Azariah	791–739
Zechariah	753		
Concluding Kings			
Shallum	752	*Jotham	752–736
Menahem	751–742		
Pekahiah	741–740	*Ahaz	(743)
Pekah	740–732		736–720
Hoshea	732/1–722	*Hezekiah	729/8–699
		Manasseh	698–643
		Amon	642–640
		Josiah	640–609
		Jehoahaz	609
		Jehoiakim	609–598
		Jehoiachin	598
		Zedekiah	597–586

* co-regency

Solomon's Temple

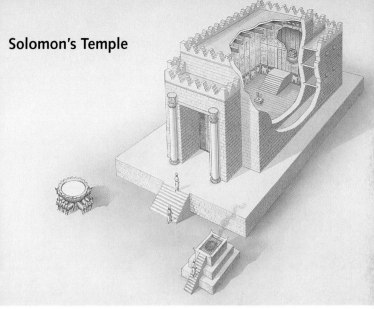

closes with the rebellion of Zedekiah against Babylon and the subsequent destruction of Jerusalem. The last event recorded is the gracious act of the king of Babylon in releasing Jehoiachin from prison (2 Kings 25:27–30).

Though the authorship of the books cannot be certainly determined, whoever wrote them had reliable written sources from which to secure material. Three written sources are named:

1. "The book of the acts of Solomon" (1 Kings 11:41)

2. "The book of the chronicles of the Kings of Judah" (1 Kings 14:29)

3. "The book of the chronicles of the Kings of Israel" (1 Kings 14:19)

4. Possibly also Isaiah (chapters 36–39).

The Talmud asserts that Jeremiah was the author. Jeremiah's prophetic ministry and his literary activity would argue in favour of this view, though someone in Babylon must have added 2 Kings 25. The certainty of his authorship, however, cannot be asserted.

The covenant, with the need for God's people to be faithful to it, is prominent in these books. The conduct of the kings is evaluated as either good or bad in the light of their fidelity to the covenant. For this reason, the prophetic thrust characterizes the books. The task of the prophets was to remind the people of their covenant obligations, to warn against idolatrous practices,

MESOPOTAMIA

Babylon

STUDY GUIDE OUTLINE TO 1 & 2 KINGS
1. The Decision to Elevate Solomon as King *1 Kings 1–4*
2. The Dedication of the Solomonic Temple
   1 Kings 5:1–9:25
3. The Deterioration of Solomon's Kingdom
   1 Kings 9:26–11:43
4. The Division of Solomon's Kingdom
   1 Kings 12–2 Kings 8
5. The Dynasty of Jehu and the Rise to Power of Israel
   2 Kings 9:1–15:12
6. The Domination of Assyrian Power
   2 Kings 15:13–21:26
7. The Decline and Captivity of Judah *2 Kings 22–25*

to convict them of their sins, and to exhort them to repentance and return to God. Failure to return to their covenant God could only result in divine judgment. The subsequent captivity underlined the people's failure to remain steadfast in obedience to the covenant.

1 & 2 Chronicles

Unique to the books of 1 and 2 Chronicles is the tracing of human history from Adam to the decree of Cyrus in 538 B.C., permitting the rebuilding of the temple of Jerusalem. Beginning with the progenitor of the human race, Adam, and narrowing down to a focus upon the three faithful tribes of Judah, Benjamin, and Levi, an accurate genealogy is provided. Such a method reveals that, in God's sight, history only had significance in Old Testament times as it related to his chosen people Israel.

This thrust is also in keeping with the purpose of the books. That the maintenance of genealogical records was the task of the priests and the priestly ministry, rather than the prophets, is heavily emphasized in these books—hence the importance of the tribe of Levi. Also Saul, Israel's first king, came from the tribe of Benjamin and, though swiftly passed over in the account, nevertheless was important to the history. David, from the Messianic tribe of Judah, was the great king of Israel to whom God gave the covenant promise of an everlasting throne and kingdom. It is with his great dynasty, his son Solomon, and the priestly courses of service in worship, especially in the Solomonic temple, that the greater part of the books deal. Only in part is any attention

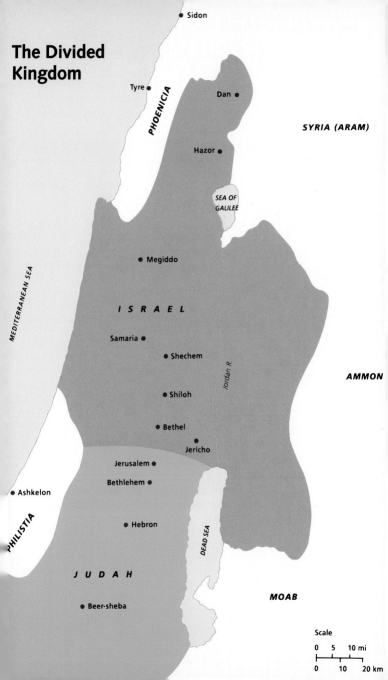

The Divided Kingdom

● Sidon

● Tyre

PHOENICIA

● Dan

SYRIA (ARAM)

● Hazor

SEA OF GALILEE

● Megiddo

I S R A E L

Samaria ●

● Shechem

Jordan R.

AMMON

● Shiloh

● Bethel

● Jericho

Jerusalem ●

Bethlehem ●

● Ashkelon

PHILISTIA

● Hebron

DEAD SEA

J U D A H

MOAB

● Beer-sheba

MEDITERRANEAN SEA

Scale

0   5   10 mi

0   10   20 km

STUDY GUIDE OUTLINE TO 1 & 2 CHRONICLES

1. The Record of David's Genealogy and Reign
   1 Chronicles
2. The Reign of Solomon *2 Chronicles 1–9*
3. The Rulers of Judah *2 Chronicles 10–36*

given to the Northern Kingdom, and that solely as it relates to the Southern Kingdom.

The title of these books, in the English form, is taken from Jerome's Latin Vulgate. Jerome translated the Hebrew title ("words of the times") as *Liber Chronicorum* (book of Chronicles). The Septuagint, or Greek Version, called it *Paraleipomenon proton kai deuteron* or "Omissions" ("things passed over") first and second. The Septuagint title possibly implies that these books record events not included in the Book of Kings.

The authorship of these books was assigned by Jewish tradition to Ezra. The subject matter and the literary style are not out of harmony with this assertion. Apart from this, the authorship of these books is uncertain. No matter who the author is, the writer of the book had an extensive number of sources available to him. The chronicler mentions or uses the following documents:

1. "The book of Samuel the seer, and in the book of Nathan the prophet, and in the book of Gad the seer" (1 Chronicles 29:29)

2. "The prophecy of Ahijah the Shilonite, and in the visions of Iddo the seer . . ." (2 Chronicles 9:29)

3. "The book of Shemaiah the prophet . . ." (2 Chronicles 12:15)

4. " . . . the book of Jehu the son of Hanani . . ." (2 Chronicles 20:34)

5. ". . . the book of the kings of Judah and Israel" (2 Chronicles 25:26)

6. "Now the rest of the acts of Hezekiah, and his goodness, behold, they are written in the vision of Isaiah the prophet . . ." (2 Chronicles 32:32)

The reference to "the book of the kings of Judah and Israel" is usually taken by scholars as a reference to a larger record of the kings, which includes data about certain wars or genealogies not included in the canonical Books of Kings. Thus, the canonical books are not a source of the chronicler's material.

Ezra & Nehemiah

Ezra and Nehemiah were originally one in the Hebrew text. The reason for this is rather obvious, since they encompass the events associated with the return of the Jews to their homeland. Together, these books give a continuous history from the decree of Cyrus in 538 B.C. (compare 2 Chronicles 36:22–23 with Ezra 1:1–4) to the final settlement of the Jews under Nehemiah, till about 430 B.C.

The Talmud states that Ezra wrote both these books. As a scribe, Ezra would be well qualified to write them. Moreover, the particular type of Aramaic utilized in 4:8–6:18 and 7:12–26 has been shown by scholars to have linguistic similarities with the Aramaic of the Elephantine papyri (fifth century B.C.), and thus is from Ezra's time. Additionally, Ezra's use of the first person in chapters 7–10 of the book of Ezra would lend weight to the view that he wrote these books.

Babylon—the place of the Jewish captivity—had just been conquered by Cyrus in 539 B.C. Following this, Darius the Mede was installed as Cyrus' governing representative. It was this Darius who raised Daniel to a place of political prominence (Daniel 5:30–6:3). Some may question, in these circumstances, why a pagan ruler like Cyrus would grant a decree permitting the repatriation of the Jews. Archaeology gives evidence, however, that Cyrus was a humane leader who sought to relocate exiles. Interestingly enough, the Scriptures (Jeremiah 25:11) declared that the Jews would only spend seventy years in Babylon. More remarkably, in his sovereign power and providence, God had predicted through Isaiah that he would use Cyrus to accomplish

This great wall in Jerusalem dates from the eighth century B.C., and was referred to by the prophet Isaiah as he addressed King Hezekiah (Isaiah 22:10).

STUDY GUIDE OUTLINE TO EZRA & NEHEMIAH

1. The Return Under Zerubbabel and Sheshbazzar
   Ezra 1–2
2. The Rebuilding of the Temple *Ezra 3–6*
3. The Religious Activity of Ezra *Ezra 7–10*
4. The Repairing of the Walls of the City *Nehemiah 1–6*
5. The Revival Under Ezra *Nehemiah 7–10*
6. The Remnant's Needs and Nehemiah's Return *Nehemiah 11–13*

his people's repatriation: "That saith of Cyrus, He is my shepherd, and shall perform all my pleasure: even saying to Jerusalem, Thou shalt be built; and to the temple, Thy foundation shall be laid" (Isaiah 44:28).

In the first return under Zerubbabel and Sheshbazzar in 538 B.C. some 42,360 Jews returned, with a vast amount of goods and animals. They began by building an altar, reinstituting the burnt offering, observing the feasts and laying the foundation of the temple. Opposition was encountered, and the building of the temple was delayed and ultimately suspended. Haggai and Zechariah exhorted them to resume building and, with Darius' decree and help, they completed the temple's building (Ezra 1–6).

An additional return of captives with Ezra took place in 457 B.C. As a scribe of the law, he taught the law, instituted reforms, and demanded a separation of the people unto God in life and practice. Personal confession of sin by Ezra for himself, and also by the people, took place. This was followed by a visible act of renewed dedication on the part of some, in putting away their foreign wives, giving evidence of their reconciliation to God's will and way.

A later return occurred under Nehemiah in 445/444 B.C., which resulted in the establishment on a more stable basis of the Jews in Palestine. This return was a result of a decree by Artaxerxes to Nehemiah to govern the city of Jerusalem and to repair the walls. Many scholars feel that this decree is also vitally important to the prophetic chronology of Daniel's seventy years (Daniel 9:24–27), as noted especially in the phrase: "Know therefore and understand, that from the going forth of the commandment to restore and to build Jerusalem unto the Messiah the Prince shall be seven weeks, and three score and two weeks; the street shall be built again, and the wall, even in troublous times" (verse 25).

Esther

Like the book of Ruth, Esther has as its main character a woman whose name is given to the book as a title. The name Esther may be derived from the Persian word for "star" or the Hebrew word for "myrtle."

MESOPOTAMIA

Susa
(Shushan)

Though the author of the book is not known, the period of history with which it deals is quite evident; it is the time when the Jews were captive in Persia. The events recorded in the book deal with the court of the Persian king at Shushan. Esther, who was Jewish but concealed it until a time of great emergency for the Jews, had become queen and was deeply loved by the Persian king. It was a providential act of God that she was queen, for through her and her relationship to Mordecai the Jews were finally delivered.

The book's historicity has been doubted but there seems no reason to doubt its authenticity. Moreover, several items clearly argue for its trustworthiness:

1. The character of the king, Ahasuerus (known by the Greek title Xerxes), as depicted in the book, matches what is known historically about him.

2. The book represents itself as historical, for it mentions the book of the Chronicles before the king (23; 6:1; 10:2).

3. The inexorability of Persian law (once a decree was issued not even a king could repeal it) is well known and explains why the only way to rescue the Jews when the day of their execution was come was to arm them and let them defend themselves, a fact that lends credibility to the killing of 75,000 Persians in one day (8:13; 9:5)

4. Archaeological confirmation came from a cuneiform in-

This depiction of a griffin was found at Susa (or Shushan), capital of the Persian Empire.

STUDY GUIDE OUTLINE TO ESTHER

1. The Decision to Make Esther Queen *1–2*
2. The Destruction of the Jews Plotted by Haman *3*
3. The Deliverance of the Jews Sought by Esther *4–7*
4. The Decimation of the Persians Accomplished *8–10*

scription listing a certain Marduk-as-a (Mordecai) as an official at the court in Shushan under Xerxes I.

The canonicity of the book has been disputed since it seems, according to some, to have no religious purpose and, more strikingly, there is no mention of the name of God in the book. Also, the evident cruelty and violence would militate against its being part of the Bible. The book, however, by its very purpose to show God's providential guidance and obvious protection of his people in a strange land is a strong argument for its canonicity. That Mordecai and Esther are strongly Jewish and monotheistic in their faith, as all Jews are, could preclude any need for God's name to be used. Also, the fact that the Jews were in a pagan, Gentile land, and that Mordecai was so careful to caution Esther about revealing her Jewishness until the proper time (3:20; 4:14), suggests that the the Jews did not want Jehovah's sacred name mentioned in the presence of Gentiles. Again, the events of this book are the basis for the renowned Jewish religious feast, the Feast of Purim, which is still celebrated. All these reasons would confirm the validity for asserting that this book has genuine credentials for its canonicity.

Essential Characteristics of Esther

1. The unusual fact that God's name is not used in the book. Many have thought such an omission incredible. But the significant providential acts, such as the choice of Esther as queen to succeed Vashti (2:15–18), the insomnia of Ahasuerus and his rewarding of Mordecai (6:1–10), and the defeat of the inexorable decree of the king (8:1–17), have no explanation apart from God's controlling power over all history.

2. The truth that the Jews are God's chosen people and his protective care over them shows that the Jews are truly distinctive and the apple of God's eye, and no one—even though many have tried throughout history—can destroy them.

3. The necessity for all believers to stand true to God in and under all kinds of circumstances. For God delivers his people out of every trial.

4. He that humbles himself God will always exalt (10:1–3).

Job

This book shares two characteristics with several other books of the Old Testament in that it belongs both to the poetical and wisdom literature of the Hebrews. The poetical books are: Job, Psalms, Proverbs, Ecclesiastes, The Song of Solomon, and Lamentations. Also Job, Proverbs, a small number of the Psalms, and Ecclesiastes are likewise classified as wisdom literature.

Hebrew Poetry

Poetry is usually difficult to translate from one language to another. It frequently loses its poetic rhythm, which is found in the sound of words. But Hebrew does not suffer too much from translation because the meaning is found in the sense of the words. Hence translations of the Bible which are poetic convey the same meaning in Hebrew and English.

The essential feature of Hebrew poetry is parallelism, according to authorities on Hebrew poetry. This parallelism is of four different classes:

1. Synonymous—the thought of line one is repeated in the second line.

2. Climactic—ascending by steps, the thought reaches a climax; Psalm 29 illustrates this.

3. Antithetical—a contrast from the thought in the first line is expressed in the second.

4. Synthetical—the first line's thought is enlarged and

Camels were owned only by rich people in Bible times. Job possessed many camels before he was tested.

completed by that of the second and any later lines.

That poetry is not unusual to Hebrew literature is evident from the contemporary literature of Israel's neighbouring nations. The Ras Shamra tablets, which contain Ugaritic literature and are similar to Hebrew, use poetry. Other languages from the same times have poetic hymns. So poetry—an age-old method of linguistic expression—is employed by God to give his divine revelation to humankind concerning our practical needs and experiences. The sighs, sobs, and songs of the human race are most vividly expressed in the language of poetry.

Wisdom Literature

Another form of biblical literature, one which also is characteristic of the contemporary literature of Israel and her neighbours, is wisdom literature. The biblical wisdom literature possesses certain characteristics: in some instances it relates to craftsmanship skills, in others to governmental management, and in yet other instances either to moral, religious, or disciplinary precepts, or to wisdom attainment as a goal of life. Such instances of wisdom literature are found in the biblical wisdom books.

In both the poetical and wisdom literature of the Old Testament, it is evident that there is a marked contrast to the same kinds of literature in contemporary literature. In the biblical literature, the teachings of divine revelation are unique and superior in every way, since they teach the need to reverence God, maintain a spiritual way of life that will glorify God, and enable us to overcome the various exigencies of life by submission to God and his leadership in our lives.

The first book fully to illustrate both poetical and wisdom literature in the Old Testament is that of Job. That he is a historical character and not a myth produced by a literary imagination to teach a moral lesson is clear from two biblical statements. He is named with two very well-known historical, personages— Noah and Daniel—as righteous men, in Ezekiel 14:14–20: "Though these three men, Noah, Daniel, and Job, were in it, they should deliver but their own souls by their righteousness, saith the Lord God . . ." James (5:11) adds his approval to Job's historicity: "Behold, we count them happy which endure. Ye have heard of the patience of Job, and have seen the end of the Lord, that the Lord is very pitiful, and of tender mercy." It would seem strange for Ezekiel and James to appeal to a mythical personage as a supreme example of righteousness and patience. Job's historicity is also attested by the factuality of the land of Uz, which was located in southeastern Edom.

Date and Authorship

The name Job means "Where is the Father?" There is some un-
certainty, however, both as to the times when the events occurred and who is the author of the book. The time when the
events took place appears to be that of the patriarchs. The arguments, while largely inferential, still make a strong case for
such times. Job must have been approximately two hundred
years old when he died, since he lived one hundred and forty
years after his illness and suffering. Such great life spans were
characteristic of the patriarchal times. Job appears to act as a high
priest—a custom in the patriarchal period. Certain characteristics of the period of the law are not mentioned, such as the law,
the tabernacle, or temple. Also, since Job depicts the care of God
in a providential way, it is rather strange—if it is of late origin
both in authorship and time—that no mention is made of God's
providential care and miraculous deliverance of Israel from Egypt.

The authorship of the book is unknown, and can never be
settled with any certainty. Depending upon one's dating of the
historical times during which the events took place, the choice
runs all the way from Job or Elihu to Moses, Solomon, or Jeremiah
to a post-exilic writer. It would be unwise to settle on any of these
dogmatically.

There are many profound teachings in this book. Hardly a
theological concept of any significance is omitted. God is the
sovereign God who is in control of the universe which he has
created and who is the rewarder of the righteous and the pun-
isher of the evil. Humanity is seen in its evil nature as well as a

The snow-
covered peaks of
Mount Hermon
in northern Israel.
One of Job's
comforters asked
him: "Were you
there when God
made the
mountains?"
(Job 15:7).

great moment of dedication, when Job acknowledges God as supreme and himself as vile. Satan is revealed as very powerful, but limited by the divine power. The theme of righteousness is also prominent, but gains significance only in relationship to God; redemption comes only from God and his grace. The teaching on the resurrection is the clearest of any teaching on the subject in the Old Testament. Job exclaimed: "For I know that my redeemer liveth, and that he shall stand at the latter day upon the earth: And though after my skin worms destroy this body, yet in my flesh shall I see God: whom I shall see for myself, and mine eyes shall behold, and not another . . ." (19:25–27).

Main Theme

The main theme of the book deals with a theodicy, that is, it seeks to answer the question of God and his relationship to evil. This is the perennial problem which humanity faces in every period of history. If God is good and all-powerful, why do the righteous suffer? Cannot God conquer evil? Why do the wicked seem always to prosper and the righteous have a very difficult time? The book, with its central discussion on the suffering of the righteous, answers this problem.

Certain background factors, unknown to the participants in the book, clouded their knowledge about Job and his problem. They did not know that Satan was testing Job with God's permission and that what he was allowed to do was limited by God. Satan was also convinced that every man had his price and if reached he would sell himself and his God out.

With this background already at hand, one's understanding of the book is greatly eased. But Job, his comforters, and Elihu had to battle their way through to that time when God put the events in perspective (Job 42).

The opening scene is set on earth with an idyllic picture of a tremendously wealthy man with a very deep devotion to God and his family. The scene then transfers to heaven, where Satan challenges God and God permits him to test Job. Back on earth, the troubles and testing of Job begin. He loses all his family and wealth, except for his wife. But through it all, Job did not lose his faith in God. His simple statement: "The LORD gave, and the LORD hath taken away; blessed be the name of the LORD" (1:21) has been a great comfort to many believers since Job's day. The verdict that "in all this Job sinned not, nor charged God with folly" portrays the phenomenal righteousness and faith of the man.

The great spiritual struggle, however, is just beginning. Struck with a painful and loathsome disease, Job curses the night of his conception and the day of his birth and longs for his death as a release from his trouble. Yet in spite of all his suffering, he maintains his integrity (chapters 1–3).

A Series of Dialogues

The main body of the book contains a series of dialogues with Job's three friends, who have come to comfort him. The gist of Eliphaz's charges (chapters 4–5) is that the wicked, not the innocent, suffer. God is faithful, therefore lay your complaint before God, accept his correction, and seek his blessing. But Job's reply (chapters 6–7) protests his innocence: "I am being crushed, show me my sin. Why does God cause a weak man to suffer?"

Bildad's contention is that God is just; only the wicked perish and, if righteous, God will restore Job. To this Job replies that an innocent man cannot contend with the omnipotent God or communicate with him—it would not avail anything; God treats all alike, both wicked and righteous. All he can do is plead with God and seek to learn the cause of his suffering (chapters 8–10).

Zophar now intervenes (chapter 11) and states that Job's boastings of innocence and righteousness are of no value before a God who knows all. Job should repent and turn to God, and then prosperity and peace will be his. To all this Job will admit no guilt (chapters 12–14). He knows God's wisdom and power better than they; none—not even God—can convict him of sin. God pursues and consumes him, and so Job cries out of the depth of discouragement: "If a man die shall he live again?"

The speeches of Job's friends continue and Job replies to each. The thrust of the speeches is the renewed charge that, since

Arab men converse in the Old City of Jerusalem. The main body of the book of Job contains a series of dialogues with Job's three friends, who came to comfort him.

STUDY GUIDE OUTLINE TO JOB

1. The Setting for Job's Suffering Described *1–3*
2. The Speeches of Job's Friends and Job's Replies Chronicled *4–31*
3. The Sovereignty of God in Man's Life in Elihu's Speech Asserted *32–37*
4. The Supremacy of God's Way in Job's Suffering and Restoration Defined *38–42*

wickedness brings suffering, Job must have sinned. Job strongly protests his innocence and states his willingness to stand before God for examination; he utters the great declaration that his innocence will be proved because "I know that my redeemer liveth, and that he shall stand at the latter day upon the earth" (19:25). Does not the fact that the wicked, though they suffer, also prosper, destroy their argument?

Job's defence concludes in the third series of speeches of his friends, who continue their debate along the same line: sin causes suffering, hence Job is guilty of secret sins. To this Job gives a biography of his life which reveals his righteousness, vindicates God's wisdom, and states that to fear him is wisdom, and then expresses a longing for a meeting with God (chapters 15–31).

At this junction, Elihu enters the debate and asserts that God does give account to man of his dealings and that he does not pervert his judgment (chapters 32–37). Job, he states, has rebelled, and any failure of God to answer prayer does not prove God's indifference but man's pride. Suffering has a divine purpose, not always known to the believer. Consider, says Elihu, the great wonders of God in nature that reveal his greatness thus: "Men do, therefore, fear him; he respecteth not any that are wise of heart."

Out of the whirlwind now comes the voice of God, who puts all in proper perspective (chapters 38–41): Consider the wonders of God in nature which manifest his greatness. Therefore, Job should not seek to usurp the position of the Almighty. Job now abases himself: "Wherefore I abhor myself, and repent in dust and ashes" (42:6). Having retracted his bitter speeches before this, Job prayed for his friends, and God then doubled his previous prosperity (chapter 42).

Psalms

Several titles have been given to Psalms, a beautiful book of songs. In the Hebrew the title is *Sepher Tephillim* which means "book of praises." Others have simply called it "praises," while the Greek Old Testament (the Septuagint) calls it *Psalmoi* from which our English translation "psalms" comes. This collection of "songs" or "praises" numbers in the Hebrew and English Bibles one hundred and fifty independent (with an exception here and there) units, or chapters. This book is the universal hymnbook of humanity. It could be called "The Sighs, Sobs, and Songs of the Human Heart." No experience of humans in their pilgrimage through this world can fail to find its expression in these profound songs or psalms. The Scottish people have put them to rhyme and they have been sung in worship services by them through the centuries.

A shepherd tends his flock in the hills outside Bethlehem. The shepherd psalm, Psalm 23, is probably the best-loved of all the psalms.

Great commentators and preachers through the history of the church have characterized the Psalms. Jerome said that "the psalms were continually to be heard in the fields and vineyards of Palestine." Ambrose noted: "Although all Divine Scripture breathes the grace of God, yet sweet beyond all others is the Book of Psalms."

In contrast to the other portions of Scripture in which God in His Word mainly speaks to the people, the Psalms instead speak on the people's behalf to God. And in the Psalms it is pointed out not *why* God should be praised but *how* God should be praised. In them also there is noted the *attributes of God* that call forth and demand *worship* (Psalms 29:2; 45:11; 95:6) and the *attitudes of humankind as* we engage in worship (Psalms 5:7; 96:9; 132:7).

The Midrash, commenting on Psalm 1:1, states: "Moses gave to the Israelites the five books of the Law, and as a counterpart to these, David gave them the Psalms, which consist of five books." The famed Hebrew and Old Testament scholar Delitzsch commented: "The Psalter is also a Pentateuch, the echo of the Mosaic Pentateuch from the heart of Israel; it is the five-fold book of the congregation to Jehovah, as the Law is the five-fold book of Jehovah to the congregation."

The Companion Bible, comparing the Pentateuch and the five books of the Psalms, comes up with the following analysis:

Book 1: Psalms 1–41
The Genesis Book deals with humankind—our blessing, rebellion, and promised redemption.
Book 2: Psalms 42–72
The Exodus Book speaks of Israel and her redemption.
Book 3: Psalms 73–89
The Leviticus Book relates to the worship of God in his sanctuary.
Book 4: Psalms 90–106
The Numbers Book centres on the people's wanderings and their pilgrimage to the final rest in God.
Book 5–Psalms 107–150
The Deuteronomy Book indicates the Word of God which restores us to God.

The book of Psalms has not one but many authors. The titles, subscriptions, and super-subscriptions to the Psalms, while not inspired, are very ancient and thus carry great weight. When ascribed to an author, it would appear that the one named is in-

STUDY GUIDE OUTLINE TO PSALMS

1. The Sons of Men: *Psalms 1–41*
   a. Humankind: *Psalms 1–8*
   b. Man of Sin: *Psalms 9–15*
   c. Man of Suffering: *Psalms 16–41*
2. The Salvation of Men and Women: *Psalms 42–72*
   a. The Nation's Sin: *Psalms 42–49*
   b. The Nation's Saviour: *Psalms 50–60*
   c. The Nation's Salvation: *Psalms 61–72*
3. The Sanctuary for Men and Women: *Psalms 73–89*
   a. The Saints and the Sanctuary: *73–83*
   b. The Saviour and the Sanctuary: *84–89*
4. The Sorrows of Men and Women: *Psalms 90–106*
   a. The Refuge from Sorrows: *Psalms 90–94*
   b. The Rejoicing in Sorrows: *Psalms 95–100*
   c. The Reigning over Sorrows: *Psalms 101–106*
5. The Surety for Men and Women: *Psalms 107–150*
   a. The Healing by the Word: *Psalms 107*
   b. The Humiliation of the Word: *Psalms 108–110*
   c. The Hallelujahs through the Word: *Psalms 111–118*
   d. The Happiness because of the Word: *Psalms 119–150*

deed the author of that Psalm. Psalms are ascribed to several authors, with David being the leading writer of some seventy-three psalms, Asaph and Korah having twelve each, while Moses and Ethan are credited with one each, and Solomon with two. Some fifty psalms have no known author.

A number of classifications have been suggested for dividing the various psalms into groups. The traditional division along this line follows:

Alphabetic or **Acrostic**: 9, 10, 25, 34, 37, 111, 112, 119, 145
Ascent: 120–134
Festal, or **Liturgical**: 113–118
Hallelujah: 106, 111–113, 117, 135, 146–150
Historical: 78, 81, 105–106, 114
Imprecatory: 35, 36, 52, 69, 109, 137
Messianic: 2, 8, 16, 22, 45, 69, 72, 89, 110, 118, 132
National: 14, 44, 46–68, 74, 76, 79–80, 83, 85, 87, 108, 122, 124–126, 129
Penitential: 6, 32, 38, 51, 130
Thanksgiving: 105, 107, 118, 136
Wisdom: 1, 16, 37, 48, 73

Proverbs

The title "The Book of Proverbs" is a translation from the title given to this book in the Vulgate, the Latin translation of the Bible. It is an apt title for a book which uses a literary device seen frequently in the ancient world, which goes back almost three thousand years before Christ.

Most scholars believe that the Hebrew word for proverbs, "*mashal*," is derived from a root word meaning "to rule," or one that means "to be like," "to be compared with." The most common form of proverb is comparison. Proverbs are generally acknowledged experiences or truths expressed in short, pithy, terse statements, or condensed parables. Supporting the idea of a condensed parable as one of the uses of a proverb is the story of Saul's prophesying: "And it came to pass, when all that knew him beforehand saw that, behold, he prophesied among the prophets, then the people said one to another, What is this that is come unto the son of Kish? Is Saul also among the prophets? And one of the same place answered and said, But who is their father? Therefore it became a proverb, Is Saul also among the prophets?" (1 Samuel 10:11–12).

The purpose of the book of Proverbs is to give instruction for life. It is to apply divine wisdom through moral rather than religious statements to the details of daily life.

This does not mean that deep theological truths are not found. Quite the contrary is true. Selecting only a few doctrinal teachings will substantiate this:

1. God is seen as creator and sustainer of the universe (3:19; 8:22).

2. God is revealed as the One who, through reverence or fear for him, is the way to knowledge and wisdom (1:7; 3:7; 9:10).

3. God is holy and will reward the righteous and condemn the wicked (3:33; 10:3; 12:2; 15:9).

4. God is all-wise and is the moral governor of the universe (10:27,29: 12:2; 15:3, 11; 21:2).

5. God is seen as Wisdom personified in reference to the pre-incarnate Christ (8:22–31). The statements in 8:22–23 show that the Lord *possessed* him *in the beginning before* his works of old. Here, no idea of creating is involved and the statement is similar to John 1:1–3.

6. God, in his relationship to the righteous as Lord of their life, seeks the evidence of practical virtues in the believers' daily acts: they are to trust in God (3:5–6), be humble (8:13), display in-

Arab women sell produce in a market near one of Jerusalem's ancient city gates. According to Proverbs, the woman is to be a model in the home, as a wife who honours her husband and a mother who guides her children.

dustry (10:4–5), evidence strength in the midst of trial (3:11–12), portray generosity towards the poor (3:27–29; 19:17), and practise justice (11:1).

7. God also lays down practical principles for the family: the father's responsibility is to lead the family through wise instruction (4:1–7); the woman is to be a model in the home as a wife who honours her husband and a mother who guides her children (31:10–31); and they are both to discipline their children lovingly and fairly (13:24; 19:18; 22:6,15; 23:13,14).

8. One of the significant lessons of this book is that, although Solomon was the wisest of men and has uttered many words of wisdom yet, as someone has said, he was a good guidepost but a poor example.

The author of most of the book of Proverbs is Solomon. According to 1 Kings 4:32, "he spoke three thousand proverbs . . ." Only

STUDY GUIDE OUTLINE TO PROVERBS
1. The Exhortations of a Father on Wisdom and Folly *1–9*
2. The Essence of Wisdom in the Fear of God *10–24*
3. The Ethical Standards of the Wise and the Foolish *25–29*
4. The Exposing of God's Word and the Fool's Arrogance *30*
5. The Excellence of a Good Mother and a Virtuous Wife *31*

about nine hundred appear in this book, however. Though from the time of Solomon (971 B.C.), yet the book was not finally compiled, according to scholars, until about 700 B.C.

The division of authorship: Solomon 1–29 (with chapters 25–29 collected by the men of Hezekiah [25:1]); Agur 30; Lemuel 31.

Ecclesiastes

The Hebrew name for Ecclesiastes is *Qoheleth* after the writer or speaker of the book (1:1,12). The Septuagint, the Greek translation of the Old Testament, names it *Ekklesiastes* and the Latin translation, the Vulgate, transliterates it *Ecclesiastes*. The English form of the title comes from this. All these words have substantially the same meaning and can be generally translated "preacher." The book has become popularly known as the book of the preacher.

The authorship of the book has been traditionally assigned to Solomon. There have been scholars—some conservative—who have argued that it does not come from Solomonic times. They do not agree as to the date of its writing. Conservative scholars date it, however, no later than the days of Malachi (about 440 B.C.), while other modern scholars put it in the Persian period, or as late as 125 B.C. Arguments to support a date later than Solomon are:

1. Prosperity characterized Solomon's days while the times of Ecclesiastes speak of tyranny and oppression.

2. The author speaks of kings in a manner that reveals he is a subject, not a king.

3. The linguistic characteristics are of a later period.

4. The philosophic traces of Stoicism (fatalism) and Epicureanism (eat, drink, be merry).

5. The reference "have gotten more wisdom than all that have been before me in Jerusalem" (1:16) must refer to kings, and

there was only one king before Solomon and that was David, so this cannot refer to Solomon.

The above arguments are not decisive against the Solomonic authorship. The reference to oppression, tyranny, and hardship are simply the vicissitudes and experiences which individuals in any period of time suffer (4:1–3; 10:6–7) and not signs of national calamity. In fact the picture of the king's wisdom, wealth, and pleasures show abundant prosperity as described in 1 Kings 4:25. As for the claim that the writer uses the past tense in referring to himself, "I was king in Jerusalem" (1:12) and thus could not be Solomon but someone impersonating him, the phrase can be translated, "I became, or have been, king in Jerusalem."

The linguistic characteristics show an affinity to early Canaanite and Phoenician linguistic phenomena and thus suit the time of Solomon. The philosophic traces of fatalism and hedonism (pleasures as the goal of life) found in 3:1–13 are not of Greek origin. They are rather exhortations to people to recognize that they are to enjoy the good life God has given them and to place each season in its proper place for God has put eternity in their hearts, "also he hath set the world ['eternity' in the Hebrew] in their heart . . ." (3:11). By being properly related to God, we can enjoy life to the full in all its seasons. All these observations indicate Solomonic authorship.

The purpose of Ecclesiastes is to demonstrate that the fullness of the good life is for humankind in submission and obedience

"Remember now thy Creator in the days of thy youth." (Ecclesiastes 12:1a).

73

to the will of God. With a right relationship to God, we can see that the temporary, impermanent, and transitory value of the good things have ultimate meaning only if God is the centre and the goal of our life and service. Thus Solomon concludes by exhorting: "Remember now thy Creator in the days of thy youth . . . Fear God, and keep his commandments . . ." (12:1a, 13a).

The Song of Solomon

There is hardly a more controversial book in the Bible than the Song of Solomon. It has run the gamut of spiritual evaluation from praise to condemnation. A Rabbinic writer has called it one of God's greatest gifts to Israel and from all the holy writings of the Old Testament has singled it out as the holy of holies. Some writers, however, have regarded it as highly erotic and lustful. Its frankness of language in the intimacy of marital relationships has been offensive to western readers, though it is in keeping with the customs of the Near-Eastern cultures of Solomon's day. A careful reading of the book will show that it guards itself delicately against any profanation of love either by eroticism or asceticism. It is a beautiful and honest picture of the purity of intimate love within the marriage bond.

The title of the book calls it a song. In the Hebrew it is called the Song of Songs and by such a phrase denotes that it is the most excellent of songs. In verse one, the phrase "which is Solomon's" gives the reason why in the English the title is the Song of Solomon. It is also the basis for the assertion of Solomonic authorship.

The authorship of Solomon has been disputed but no substantial arguments have been advanced which are compelling enough to give up the traditional view. The geographic locale and descriptions associated with it are Palestinian and Solomonic. Also, though some have asserted that there are Greek loan-words, other scholars have denied this. Such loan-words would not negate the authorship by Solomon since there were many commercial contacts with other countries in his day.

A quiet spot in Jerusalem's Garden of Gethsemane. The writer of The Song of Solomon uses the imagery of the garden.

STUDY GUIDE OUTLINE TO THE SONG OF SOLOMON

1. The Dialogues of the Bride and Bridegroom *1:1–3:6*
2. The Decision of the Bride to Accept the Bridegroom's Invitation *3:7–5: 1*
3. The Dreams of the Bride about the Bridegroom's Departure *5:2–6:3*
4. The Delight of the Bride and Bridegroom in Their Love *6:4–8:14*

The purpose of the book is to portray an actual relationship between Solomon and the Shulamite maiden. This experience reveals the purity of love in the most intimate marital relationships and pictures figuratively the loving relationship between God and Israel as husband and wife and Christ and the church as bridegroom and bride (compare Hosea 2:19–20; Ephesians 5:25–33).

Two other methods of interpretation of this book do not appear to do justice to its meaning. The allegorical method denies any authenticity to the story and makes it a purely spiritual depiction of Solomon as representative of God and the Shulamite as Israel. The literal method makes it a historical event with no spiritual significance.

The Prophets

The order of the prophetic books of the Old Testament includes the last seventeen books from Isaiah through Malachi. They are generally divided into the major and minor prophets. This division comes not from the importance of the books but from their size. In the Hebrew Bible the minor prophets, because of their size, were preserved in one scroll to guard against loss or destruction.

The prophetic ministry in the Old Testament times was vital and necessary for God's people. The prophet took God's message and delivered it to the people. It was usually a message of judgment, but always one filled with God's redemptive love and grace. Such a ministry is in contrast to the priestly one. The priest stands between the people and God; the prophet stands between God and the people.

In the prophetic books will be found God's warnings concerning impending judgment, with the command to repent and to seek forgiveness. God stands always ready to receive the repentant nation. If repentance is not manifested, then punishment will fall; but ultimately, restoration will come. For in the message of gloom and doom, there is always the gleaming ray of hope.

The Prophets and their Message

Isaiah to Malachi Period c. 800–400 B.C.

To Israel before the fall of the northern kingdom, 722 B.C.	To Judah during her declining years.	To Judah in her last years, 634–606 B.C.	To exiles in Babylon, 606–538 B.C.	To restored community, 538–400 B.C.
Amos Divine punishment follows persistent sin.	**Joel*** The Day of the Lord and Judgment of nations.	**Jeremiah** Jerusalem's judgment and coming glory	**Daniel** The times of the Gentiles and Israel's kingdom	**Haggai** Restoration of temple and kingdom foretold.
Hosea God's love for Israel.	**Obadiah*** Doom upon Edom.	**Nahum** Doom of Nineveh and Assyria.	**Ezekiel** Future restoration of Israel and the land.	**Zechariah** Messiah the branch and king–priest.
Jonah Nineveh, repent! God's concern for Gentiles.	**Isaiah** The coming Saviour and Israel's king.	**Habakkuk** The Lord's kingdom and people will triumph.		**Malachi** Final judgment and warning to the nation.
	Micah Bethlehem's king and kingdom.	**Zephaniah** Remnant rescued for blessing.		

* since these prophets do not specifically date their ministries, opinions vary as to where they should be placed.

Isaiah

The name Isaiah comes from the prophet who wrote the book. Our English title, therefore, is a transliteration of the shorter Hebrew form of the word *Isaiah*. The name Isaiah means "Jehovah is salvation."

The prophet Isaiah was the son of Amoz, and tradition states that he was of royal lineage—his father was reputed to be the brother of King Amaziah. This would make Isaiah a first cousin of King Uzziah. It was in the year of this king's death, about 740 B.C., that Isaiah probably commenced his ministry. His ministry continued for approximately sixty years and ended in martyrdom, according to tradition, by being sawn asunder (Hebrews 11:37) during the reign of the wicked King Manasseh, about 680 B.C.

The meaning of the names of Isaiah and his two children appear to be a summation of the events and teaching of this book. The major thrust of Isaiah's message is the supernatural power of God to deliver (Jehovah is salvation) in every circumstance—temporal or spiritual. The name Maher-shalal-hash-baz (haste the booty, haste the spoil) signifies the speedy deliverance of Jerusalem from the siege by Syria and Ephraim through the agency of Assyria who despoiled them. The Assyrians carried these people away as captives. This action portended the inevitable and inexorable captivity which would befall Judah. The name of Shear-jashub (a remnant shall return) reveals that God will not

Isaiah describes Israel as God's vineyard, which he has planted with the best stock.

forget his people but restoration and a return to the land will come.

This book, which has suffered so much at the hands of the higher critics, is one of the most profound, sublime, and remarkable books of all of the Old Testament prophetic books. It is the gospel before the gospel. It is the revelation of God's government and grace before its final interpretation in Christ. The mercy, grace, love, and justice of God are fully shown in this book. So remarkable are the great themes of Isaiah that when Augustine was converted and asked Ambrose which of the sacred books he should begin to study, he replied: "The prophecies of Isaiah!" Such is this great book of Isaiah.

The almost universal testimony of both Jewish and Christian tradition has been that Isaiah is the author of the entire book. Higher critical scholars assert, on the contrary, that there were a number of authors. Basically, however, these can be reduced to two divisions of the book, which have been generally known as First Isaiah and Deutero, or Second, Isaiah. To Isaiah would belong chapters 1–39 and to Deutero-Isaiah, chapters 40–66.

Arguments Against the Unity of Isaianic Authorship

1. The literary differences between the two sections.

2. The chronological distinctions between the two sections reveal that the last part (40–66) was written during the Babylonian captivity and are thus future to the time of Isaiah.

3. The differing theological and subject content between the two divisions.

Competent conservative scholars have shown through extensive research that these arguments can be adequately answered. The main distinction between the traditional view of Isaianic authorship and the critical multiple authorship is in the presupposition with which one approaches the book. The higher critic rejects, while the conservative scholar accepts, futuristic prophecy. This will account, therefore, for the last portion of Isaiah as Babylonian in character. It is a prophetic picture of the exilic conditions in Babylon which reveals Israel's deliverance through Cyrus, the Persian king (a prophecy fulfilled one hundred and fifty years later). Like John on Patmos, Isaiah prophesied the exile and also Israel's future glory. As to the literary style, the Hebrew of both sections is pure and shares the same characteristics. The theological and subject content are tied together with the oft-recurring phrase of both parts—the Lord is "The Holy One of Israel." This phrase occurs twelve times in the first part and thirteen times in the second.

Jerusalem •

Evidence for Unity and Authenticity

1. The witness of Ecclesiasticus, the son of Sirach, about 180 B.C., who noted Isaiah's comfort of God's people (an allusion to Isaiah 40:1) and who did not speak of any other prophet in the exilic period as the writer of this section.

2. The famed Isaiah Scroll of the Dead Sea Scrolls, which gives no hint of any knowledge of a break between the two major divisions of Isaiah.

3. The witness of Christ and the apostles, who identified, through quotations, both portions as being from Isaiah (compare John 12:38–41 with Isaiah 53:1 and 6:9, 10).

The author of this book shows that by family relationship (royal descent) and educational background he was well qualified to write a profound and prophetic book. He had access to the centre of government (Isaiah 6) and an intimate knowledge of Jerusalem, Palestine, surrounding nations, and world history. His literary style was superb, his diction clear, his poetry passionate, and his oratory skilfully stirring.

The character of the times was one of flux and change. Assyria had come to life under Tiglath Pileser III (745–27) and then later under Sennacherib (705–681), Palestine was invaded, and all the major cities of Palestine, with the exception of Jerusalem, were levelled. Babylon commenced to move as a power among the nations, and in one hundred years became the world's greatest empire. Syria's end came about with Assyria's defeat of Rezin. Rome, which would one day rule Palestine, was founded just a

A distant view of the Old City of Jerusalem. The prophet Isaiah delivered a severe judgment on the city.

STUDY GUIDE OUTLINE TO ISAIAH

1. The Condemnation of Judah and Jerusalem *1–12*
2. The Concern of the Prophet with the Surrounding Nations *13–23*
3. The Consummation of Kingdom Promises Predicted *24–27*
4. The Characteristic Warnings Against the Futility in Seeking Alliances *28–35*
5. The Curing of Hezekiah *36–39*
6. The Comforting and Consummating Prophecies Delivered *40–66*

few years after Isaiah's birth, and the Greek city-states were beginning to blossom. Anxiety and restlessness, therefore, were the order of the day.

The social conditions were atrocious. The poor became poorer as the rich grabbed land illegally and forced out of their homes by extortion and eviction home-owners who could not meet their payments. Government and the judicial system were horribly corrupt, taking bribes under the table to favour the wealthy.

Moral conditions were characterized by licentiousness, drunkenness, moral indifference, idolatrous worship, and religious prostitution. The Moloch worship rite, with the sacrifice of the first born, was prevalent.

It was into such a period that Isaiah entered, with his ministry of denunciation of the sins of the people, his proclamation of the sovereign holiness of God, and his warnings of impending judgment unless repentance and forsaking of sin were quickly exercised.

Concepts of Isaiah's Message That Made His Ministry Unique and Necessary

1. God is the Holy One of Israel and he cannot tolerate evil and wickedness (1:4; 30:12–14; 41:14; 55:5; 60:9, 14).

2. Human beings are wicked and evil and in need of redemption (6:5–7).

3. God will preserve a remnant and will restore that remnant (1:9; 11:11; 16:14; 46:3). The remnant, faithful to the Lord, is very important to Isaiah's message of judgment and comfort.

4. The great prophecies relating to Christ are comprehensive and unusual: his birth (7:14; 9:6), his deity (9:6–7), his death (52:13–53:12).

A Jew in his prayer shawl blows a ram's horn trumpet at Jerusalem's Western Wall. Isaiah proclaimed that a trumpet would summon God's people from exile (Isaiah 27).

5. The concept of the servant of the Lord is two-fold. In some instances it refers to Christ (11:2; 42:1–3; 50:5–6; 52:13–15; 53:1–13; 65:8) and in others to Israel (41:8; 43:10; 44:1–2; 45:4).

6. God will establish his kingdom at the end of history and the Messiah will reign (chapters 2; 11; 65).

Jeremiah

The prophet Jeremiah, who gave his name to this book, lived and ministered in Judah during the times of heartache and sorrow for the nation. A swift spiritual decline characterized the people who descended from the heights of revival under Josiah to apostasy and exile under Jehoiachin and Zedekiah.

The political conditions which ultimately brought about the downfall of Jerusalem and Judah saw the decline of Assyrian power with the destruction of Nineveh in 612 B.C., and the defeat of the Egyptians by the Babylonians at the battle of Carchemish in 605 B.C. This battle, one of the pivotal points in Old Testament history, opened up western Asia to the dominance of Babylon. In 597 B.C. the Babylonians appeared at the gates of Jerusalem for a second time and captured Jehoiachin, leading him and some 10,000 of his people as captives to Babylon (2 Kings 24:14). The final onslaught of the Babylonians against Jerusalem took place eleven years later (586 B.C.).

Despite the continued pleas of Jeremiah for the king and people to surrender to Babylon, they sought to withstand the siege, but finally had to capitulate; total destruction of the city and temple followed.

The ministry of Jeremiah (whose name means "Yahweh appoints" or "establishes" or "exalts") occupied at least some forty-one years from 627 B.C. During these years the prophet suffered personal humiliation (20:1–3), persecution (27:1–15), and rejection by his own people. Jeremiah's great love for his people never wavered and with a heart filled with compassion, often weeping as he spoke, he sought to halt the rushing stream of apostasy and prevent divine judgment by calling for national repentance. The people, however, continued their spiritual plunge towards inevitable captivity. The year 586 B.C. marked this deadline. Jeremiah probably closed his ministry in Egypt, where he was taken by the remnant of the Jews, following the destruction of Jerusalem (43:6–7).

The authorship of this book has been traditionally assigned to Jeremiah. There is no need to deny this. Jeremiah had a secretary named Baruch, who recorded the messages of Jeremiah and the events associated with his ministry. The book speaks of instances where Jeremiah and Baruch were commanded to write certain events down (30:1; 36:2–4; 45:1; 51:60). In all probability chapter 52 was added later (compare 2 Kings 25:1–26).

STUDY GUIDE OUTLINE TO JEREMIAH

1. The Commission of the Prophet *1*
2. The Condition of the People in Sinfulness *2–6*
3. The Call to the People to Repent *7–12*
4. The Certainty of Captivity for the People *13–18*
5. The Confrontation of the Prophet with the Leaders *19–29*
6. The Covenant Promise of Restoration *30–33*
7. The Catastrophic Events Relating to Judah and the Nations *34–52*

Highlights of Jeremiah's Teaching

1. God is creator (10:12; 27:5), governor (5:22, 24; 23:23), omniscient (17:9–10), Saviour (2:13; 17:13–14).

2. God demands obedience to the moral law (6:19) prior to the observance of the ceremonial law (6:20). Obedience to ceremonies does not take the place of obedience to the moral law.

3. God's call to a person places upon them a burden to discharge that calling from which they cannot escape (20:9).

4. God's servant must have the courage to declare divine judgment upon an unrepentant people, regardless of the consequences (37:16–21).

5. God's servant must be compassionate as he or she delivers the message of God's condemnation and impending judgment (13:15–27).

6. God does not forget his people, but will fulfil his covenant promises. The exile would not be forever, but restoration would come at the end of seventy years (25:11–14). These covenant promises extend to the end time, when the Messiah will establish his kingdom (23:58; 31:31–34).

7. God's servant should be willing to put his or her faith in God's promises to the test in order to strengthen God's people and lead them to obedience (32:6–15).

Since the oracles of Jeremiah were not delivered in chronological sequence, it is difficult to analyze the book under any system of general subjects.

Lamentations

The name Lamentations is derived from the title given to it in the Greek Version of the Old Testament, the Septuagint. The Greek word is *threnoi*, meaning "Lamentations." In the Hebrew the title comes from the first word in chapters one, two, and four. This word means literally, "Ah, how!"

The book consists of five elegies—meditative poems of lamentations of sorrow relating usually to death. The first four elegies are cast in the form of funeral laments or dirges. The fifth elegy is basically a prayer of contrition and confession by the people for their sins (5:7), as well as a vindication of God's justice and a call for mercy: "Turn thou us unto thee, O LORD, and we shall be turned; renew our days as of old. But thou hast utterly rejected us; thou art very wroth against us" (5:21–22).

These elegies are written predominantly in a literary style that is called an acrostic, or alphabetic, arrangement. This style was originally adopted as a memory device to enable the reader to remember the material. The arrangement of the stanzas in the first three elegies consists of three lines each with the exception of 1:7 and 2:9, which have four lines each. Each of these stanzas begins with a letter of the Hebrew alphabet in regular sequence. There are two letters of the Hebrew alphabet, however, which are inverted (*ayin* and *pe*) in three instances: 2:16–17; 3:46–51; 4:16–17. The third elegy, however, differs slightly from the others by having each line of each three-line stanza begin with the same Hebrew letter. Though consisting of twenty-two stanzas (the same number as the letters of the Hebrew alphabet), the fifth elegy does not follow the alphabetic arrangement. Elegies four and five also differ from the first three in having only two-line rather than three-line stanzas.

From early times, the tradition of the church has been to attribute authorship of this book to Jeremiah. Recent scholarship, however, has questioned this tradition. The historical events and the literary features and style of the books of both Jeremiah and Lamentations argue for identity of authorship by Jeremiah. A study of the following similar features of the two books strongly reinforces this identity:

1. The vivid recording of Jerusalem's fate.

2. The weeping and lamentation of the prophet over his people's sins.

3. The prophet's deep conviction that God will punish his people's enemies.

The ruins of an old synagogue in Jerusalem. Jeremiah lamented over the fall of his beloved city of Jerusalem.

STUDY GUIDE OUTLINE TO LAMENTATIONS

1. The Cry of the City Uttered *1*
2. The Chastisement of the City Deserved *2*
3. The Contrition of the City Counselled *3*
4. The Calamitous Horrors of the City Delineated *4*
5. The Confession and Prayer of the City Described *5*

4. The abiding hope of the prophet that, in the future, God will forgive and restore his people.

The purpose of the book is to record Jeremiah's lament over his beloved city of Jerusalem, a lament which foreshadows the lament of the Saviour over Jerusalem (Luke 13:34).

Ezekiel

Ezekiel is named after the prophet, the son of Buzi and of a priestly family (1:3). Carried to Babylon as a captive eleven years before the destruction of Jerusalem, he was approximately twenty-five years of age when called to the prophetic ministry. His name means "God will strengthen" or "God will prevail." His ministry covered the years 593–571 B.C. He was, thus, a contemporary of Daniel in Babylon and of Jeremiah, who remained in Jerusalem.

Both Daniel and Ezekiel resided in Babylon: Daniel in the city, Ezekiel in the country. Both were prophets, though Daniel was also a governmental official. The ministry of Daniel was to counsel the nations under whom the Jews lived; that of Ezekiel to comfort the exiles.

The prophetic messages of both Jeremiah and Ezekiel shared a common theme: the impending fall and destruction of Jerusalem. Upon hearing the news that Jerusalem had fallen, Ezekiel changed his prophetic proclamations to those of hope, encouragement, and the ultimate restoration for God's people. He did not live to see the return to Palestine of his people fulfilled; the decree for their restoration came some thirty years after his death.

The authorship of the book by the prophet Ezekiel was the unanimous tradition of the church. But the advent of higher criticism brought with it the denial of both the unity and Ezekiel's authorship of the book. The uniqueness of Ezekiel's language, the unquestioned evidence of Ezekiel's life before the destruction of the temple, and the priestly and historical allusions all reinforce the church's tradition that Ezekiel was the author.

Striking Symbols and Parables Employed in Ezekiel

1. The symbols and signs under which Ezekiel received and conveyed God's revelation give the book, therefore, much in common with Revelation (compare Ezekiel 1:4–12 with Revelation 4:6–8; Ezekiel 10:1–7 with Revelation 8:1–5).

2. The shekinah glory, which indicated the presence of God among his people, is important in Ezekiel (1:28; 3:23; 8:4; 9:3; 10:4,18; 11:22–23; 43:2–5). The departure of the glory of the Lord was gradual, going from the temple, then the city, and finally from the Mount of Olives. This means that God was reluctant to leave his people, but their wickedness demanded it. Though patient and longsuffering, God must finally let his judgment fall.

3. The concept of remnant is also vital to Ezekiel's teaching.

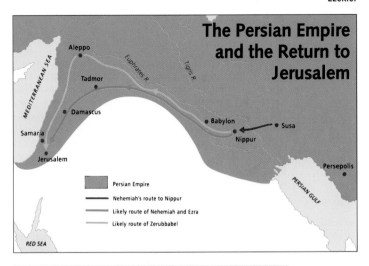

The Persian Empire and the Return to Jerusalem

Persian Empire
Nehemiah's route to Nippur
Likely route of Nehemiah and Ezra
Likely route of Zerubbabel

STUDY GUIDE OUTLINE TO EZEKIEL

1. The Prophet Ezekiel's Commission *1–3*
2. The Proclamation of the City's Guilt and Doom *4–24*
3. The Prophecies against the Foreign Countries *25–32*
4. The Promises Concerning Restoration *32–39*
5. The Portrait of the Temple and Land *40–48*

God has always left a remnant. In this case, the remnant will know why God's chastening hand has fallen upon his people (6:10,14).

4. The graphic and poignant story of the death of Ezekiel's wife reveals how costly the prophetic office could be. Like Hosea, Ezekiel was chosen to depict the relationship between God and his people. Death dissolved the marriage of Ezekiel and his wife; the destruction of Jerusalem would dissolve (though only temporarily) the relationship between God and his people.

5. Using the King of Tyre as a visible example, God portrays the source of evil behind world government. This symbolism also reveals the way in which evil came into the universe (compare Isaiah 14:12–14).

6. The national resurrection of Israel is vividly expressed in Ezekiel 37:1–28.

7. The remarkable picture of the temple for restored Israel is contained in chapters 40–48.

Daniel

In the Hebrew Bible, Daniel is included in the "Writings," though the Lord Jesus called Daniel a prophet: "When ye therefore, shall see the abomination of desolation, spoken of by Daniel the prophet, stand in the holy place . . ." (Matthew 24:15). The book's title comes from its major figure, Daniel, whose name means "God is my judge." In the English Bible, however, Daniel is found among the major prophets. The reason is not only that Christ called him "the prophet," but that his book is filled with prophetic predictions. Some of the most important prophecies in the Old Testament come from the inspired pen of Daniel: the outline of world history (2:36–45), the Seventy Weeks (9:24–27), the Wars of the Ptolemies and Seleucids (11:1–35), and the deliverance of Israel (12:1–13).

The book is largely apocalyptic in nature. Such literature differed from ordinary prophetic writings in its use of symbols, which were given through the vehicle of dreams and visions. Biblical apocalyptic is also distinct in that the prophecies are literal and real. They are not simply spiritual truths couched in symbolic forms because they reflect well the true meaning of *apocalupsis*, meaning "revelation." Nothing is hid as in apocrypha (that is, the hidden [non-canonical] books). The very character of apocalyptic literature declares that a symbol cannot symbolize a symbol (thus be purely spiritual in nature); it must stand for that which is real. Apocalyptic is also distinct from regular prophetic utterances in that it is world-embracing in coverage.

The historical background is the time of the Babylonian exile. Daniel is with his people in captivity, having been taken there under Nebuchadnezzar in 605 B.C. Maintaining a scrupulous and faithful witness during his time in captivity, Daniel suffered much. But God elevated him to the second most important governmental position, a position he is still holding under the Persians as the book closes (6:1–3; 12:8–13). Many critics, however, have denied such an appointment by the Persian King Darius the Mede, because no secular historical record has mentioned a king by this precise name. Competent scholars, however, have shown that this Darius may be identified either with Gobyras, governor of Babylon, under Cyrus, or Cyrus himself.

Like Daniel, the book of Daniel has had its own "den of lions" experience. Modern critics contend that the book is falsely ascribed to Daniel and comes from the time of the Maccabees in 165 B.C., being written to encourage the Jews during their fierce

STUDY GUIDE OUTLINE TO DANIEL

1. The Setting of the Book Historically *1*
2. The Scope of Gentile World History *2–7*
3. The Saints of God and Their Relationship to the Consummation of World History *8–12*

Relief of a lion and lioness from Nineveh. Like Daniel, the book of Daniel has had its own "den of lions" experience.

struggle with Antiochus Epiphanes. The traditional view of the authorship of the book is that Daniel wrote it, and it comes from the sixth century. As noted above, arguments from history, linguistics, purpose, and exegesis have been levelled against both the time and the authorship of Daniel. Though formidable, these arguments have been answered by conservative scholars and there is no need to deny Daniel's authorship. One's attitude towards predictive prophecy plays a great part in settling the questions of authorship. But the writing of the book cannot be brought down far enough in time to deny prophecy, since it predicts Christ's coming.

The book is written in two languages and is distinctive for the use of the languages. The Hebrew relates God's dealings with his own people, and the Aramaic (the language of diplomacy in that day) relates to the Gentile world powers as they are seen in God's plan for his people to the end of time.

Hosea

Hosea, the son of Beeri, had a unique ministry as a prophet who had to suffer shame, heartbreak, and domestic sorrow in order to teach God's people a vital spiritual lesson—a lesson symbolized by his marital situation, which God uses to portray his own undying love for his people. It is a profound love story of a prophet who was willing to undergo all the traumas of infidelity and desertion in marriage in order to impress God's continuing fidelity to a faithless and adulterous people.

In this story, which reaches the profoundest depths of pathos, there unfolds a most remarkable love story, a story equal to that contained in John 3:16. The love of God cannot be measured. Though his people wander far from him and revel in wickedness, God will not forsake them forever. He will search and seek for them and upon their repentance and return will restore them to his favour.

The meanings of the names of the prophet and his children have spiritual significance as the story unfolds. Hosea, whose name means "salvation," reveals through his name that God will ultimately restore and bless Israel. Jezreel's name means "the Lord sows, or scatters." This child's name portends the impending judgment of Jeroboam II (a descendant of Jehu) and also looks back upon the events associated with the blood of Jezreel shed by Jehu (1 Kings 19:15–17; 2 Kings 10:1–14). In this judgment upon Jeroboam II, God will not show mercy as the name Lo-ruhamah ("unpitied") indicates. The rejection of God's people is solemnly stated in Lo-ammi ("not my people"). This graphic portrayal through these names of God's message prophetically underscored for Israel the inevitability of divine retribution.

Hosea's ministry, emphasizing this message, took place during the reigns of Uzziah, Jotham, Ahaz, and Hezekiah, Kings of Judah, and Jeroboam II, King of Israel. Contemporary prophets during his ministry were Amos in Israel, and Isaiah and Micah in Judah. The dates usually assigned to Hosea are 770–725 B.C.

Those who have challenged the unity of the book and its authorship by Hosea usually cite passages that mention Judah, and verses such as 4:3, 9; 7:10; 11:8–11, and 14:2–9. An understanding of predictive prophecy and a realization that God will ultimately restore Israel would answer most of these criticisms and leave Hosea's authorship intact.

The critical problem of the prophecy relates to the sovereign holiness of God and the command of God to Hosea: ". . . And

STUDY GUIDE OUTLINE TO HOSEA

1. The Charge Against Israel *1–3*
2. The Corruption of Israel *4:1–6:3*
3. The Condemnation of Israel *6:4–11:4*
4. The Conversion of Israel *11:5–14:9*

the LORD said to Hosea, Go, take unto thee a wife of whoredoms and the children of whoredoms . . ." (1:2). Did God really direct Hosea to commit immorality? Would he want to teach a vivid lesson to Israel of her spiritual adultery by commanding a prophet to marry a harlot?

Three Possible Interpretations

1. The *symbolic* view says that the marriage never actually took place. God used this as a symbolic method to reveal to Israel her infidelity and adulteries.

2. The *realistic* view says that Hosea married a harlot—a woman he knew to be an unchaste woman.

3. The *prophetic* view says that the prophet interpreted his own life prophetically in the light of after events as under God's providential guidance, and that unconsciously he had married a woman *destined* to be a harlot and bear children of harlotry. Or, it could be that Hosea knew (as did God) that his wife would become a harlot (as Israel would).

This last view appears to be the best one. It supports the plainest and simplest meaning of the passage. Other scriptural instances show where a literal event took place and its meaning only became clear later (Jeremiah 32:7; Ezekiel 24:15ff.). Such an interpretation preserves God from condoning sin or causing a sinful act by the prophet, and also saves Hosea from a poor testimony as he illustrates, in his marriage, the case of Israel's spiritual adultery from Jehovah. Additionally, it is the best conclusion to draw from 1:2 and 2:5–7.

The early part of Joel describes a terrible invasion of locusts, symbolizing the coming Day of the Lord.

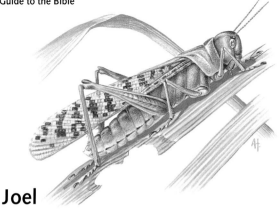

Joel

The name Joel means "Jehovah is God" and occurs some fourteen times in the Old Testament. The son of Pethuel ("persuaded of God"), Joel was in all probability a native of Judah, and well acquainted with Jerusalem (2:1, 23; 3:1, 6). From the references to the temple, he was possibly a priest as well as a prophet in the fullest meaning of the word (1:1).

The date of the book is debated. Some put it during the time of Uzziah about 770 B.C., while others put it during the post-exilic times about 432 B.C. The earlier date seems preferable. Its position in the canon between Hosea and Amos, its literary style, similar to Amos (who appears to have quoted from Joel 3:16 (Amos 1:2) and Joel 13:8 (Amos 9:13), its historical circumstances, which do not reflect the negligent and apathetic post-exilic days, and the enemies of Judah, Phoenicians (3:4), Egypt, and Edom (3:19), argue strongly for the earlier date.

Using a severe locust plague as a warning of impending judgment, the prophet calls the people to repentance and a return to God before it falls. He also uses this occasion to pronounce a greater and severer judgment: "the day of the Lord" is coming. The Holy Spirit will be poured out before that great and terrible day (2:28–32). Peter shows the fulfilment of this, but not its full consummation, on the day of Pentecost (Acts 2:16).

STUDY GUIDE OUTLINE TO JOEL

1. The Characteristics of the Day *1*
2. The Chastisement of the Day *2:1–27*
3. The Consummation of the Day *2:28–3:21*

Amos

A native of Tekoa in Judah, Amos was called by God to minister to the Northern Kingdom. His name means "burden" or "burden-bearer." Since his father's name is not mentioned, he came from the poorer class. The circumstances of his call would also indicate this (7:10–17). God called him from tending sheep and cultivating wild fig trees. He had an unshakeable conviction of his divine call, and nothing would deter him from delivering his burden or message.

Tekoa •

Amos' times were times of political tranquillity and peace, economic wealth, social luxury, ruthless capitalism, judicial corruption, and moral depravity. Religious formalism and ritualism, which combined idolatry with the worship of Jehovah, was the order of the day. The holiness of God was blasphemed (4:2), the commandments of God were violated (2:4–8), and their position as God's chosen people was despised (3:2). These all combined to undermine the spiritual and ethical responsibilities of the people and to call down God's proclamation of imminent judgment upon them.

The design of the book, therefore, is to point out God's goodness to the people and to warn them that, because of their wickedness, God would severely punish them unless they repented. To those who are faithful and fear God, a day of bright hope, with its social and economic security will come, when the tabernacle or kingdom of David is re-established (9:11–15).

Most scholars agree that the book is a unity and that Amos is the author.

STUDY GUIDE OUTLINE TO AMOS

1. The Condemned Nations *1–2*
2. The Chosen Nation *3–6*
3. The Comforted Nation *7–9*

Obadiah

Obadiah is the shortest yet one of the most profound prophetic books in the Old Testament. It deals with the doctrine of sin and its awful consequences as portrayed in the lives of two nations—Israel and Edom, who were cousins. Obadiah, whose name means "servant, or worshipper, of Jehovah," is the author of the book. There seems to be no strong reason to doubt this, though some critics view the book as a collection of oracles. Their reason for doing so is, in part, a rejection of predictive prophecy, such as found in verses 17–21.

Since it is not possible to connect Obadiah with any of the other Obadiahs mentioned in the Old Testament, it is difficult to date the time of his ministry. Many scholars look upon Obadiah as the earliest of the writing prophets and the Edomite invasion of Judah during the reign of Jehoram (848–841 B.C.) as the occasion for the prophecy.

Locked into what it considered an impregnable fortress city and controlling the trade route from Gaza to Damascus, Edom would make frequent raids upon the business caravans travelling this route as well as periodic invasions of Judah (2 Chronicles 21:16–17; 2 Kings 8:20). These were but the continuing signs of the hostility between the two nations of Israel and Edom, which began in the womb of Rebekah (Genesis 25:19–34) and continued as occasion presented itself, as in the Exodus wanderings (Numbers 20:14–21).

The design of the book is to reveal that Edom's hatred of, and violence toward, God's people will be punished. The doom, destruction, and final extinction of Edom are predicted.

Lessons to be learned in Obadiah

1. God is the Lord of history and his purpose will be fulfilled.
2. Pride is selfishness manifested and is the essential principle of sin.
3. Sin brings violence and retribution.
4. God remembers his own in their trials and restores them in his own time.

STUDY GUIDE OUTLINE TO OBADIAH

1. The Rebellion of Edom Perceived *1–6*
2. The Ruin of Edom Predicted *7–16*
3. The Restoration of Israel Promised *17–21*

Jonah

Jonah is probably one of the best known of the minor prophets because of the miraculous event recorded—an event which is incredible to many, but to those who believe in God's supernatural power, it is not impossible. Apart from recorded instances in history and today where people have been swallowed by great fishes and lived, the testimony of Christ as to the authenticity and historicity of the events places them beyond denial for the believer (Matthew 12:39–40).

Jaffa *(Joppa)*

The truly miraculous event of the book is the repentance of Nineveh and her forgiveness by God. Jonah was aware of God's graciousness, love, and mercy and that, should Nineveh repent, God would withhold his judgment (4:2). This is why Jonah fled towards Tarshish. Like all Israel, he hated Nineveh because of the unusual and inhuman cruelties and atrocities visited upon her enemies. Jonah would have delighted in her complete extermination!

There is little known about Jonah, whose name means "dove." Some have identified him with the Jonah, the son of Amittai, in 2 Kings 14:25. If so, this would place Jonah's ministry about 760–755 B.C.

The book teaches the sovereign providence of God as he reveals his mercy, love, grace, and forgiveness towards the repentant sinner.

The Mediterranean Sea viewed from Jaffa—biblical Joppa. When God sent Jonah to Nineveh, he went instead to the port of Joppa.

STUDY GUIDE OUTLINE TO JONAH

1. The Command to Jonah *1*
2. The Confession of Jonah *2*
3. The Commission to Jonah *3*
4. The Controversy with Jonah *4*

Micah

Micah's ministry can be dated from the kings mentioned in 1:1, and would thus fall within the years 738–698 B.C. The prophet's name means "Who is like Jehovah?" He was a native of Moresheth and a citizen of the Southern Kingdom of Judah.

The book's unity and authorship have been questioned by critics. They contend that certain ideas are out of harmony with Micah's times. Thus, it must be a compilation with an editorial appendix in 7:7–20. Micah, however, was contemporaneous with Isaiah and Hosea, and ideas similar to his can be found in their books (compare, for instance, his prophecy of the destruction of Judah [Micah 1:9–16] with Hosea 5:10; Isaiah 6:11–13). Hence, there is no reason to deny his authorship.

The political situation in Micah's day was one of great unrest, and the international scene among the nations was changing rapidly. Assyria was on the rise, and Israel fell to her conquering armies in 722 B.C. and was held captive. Judah, under God's providential care, was spared from the Assyrians on three occasions. The last of these was a siege of Jerusalem by Sennacherib, from which the city, because of Hezekiah's prayer and faithful dedication, gained a miraculous deliverance when the angel of death killed 185,000 Assyrian soldiers (2 Kings 19:35).

Social conditions of the times saw judges corrupt, priests immoral, prophets mere professionals, and the greed for money rampant and unmanageable. Religiously, people had itching ears (2:11), prophet and priest fought to maintain their luxurious lifestyles (3:5), and honesty and integrity were at the vanishing point. Pagan religious practices were still widespread in the land.

Amidst such conditions, Micah predicts impending judgment upon both Israel and Judah. The prophetic message never closes without a promise of hope, for in the last days the kingdom will be established under the majestic Messiah (4:1–13), whose birthplace for his first advent is predicted (5:2).

Moresheth

•

STUDY GUIDE OUTLINE TO MICAH

1. The Charge Against Israel *1–2*
2. The Concern for Israel *3–5*
3. The Controversy with Israel *6:1–7:6*
4. The Confidence of Israel *7:7–20*

Young Jews rejoice in the streets of Jerusalem. Micah looked forward to a time when God's people would return rejoicing to the Holy City.

Nahum

Nahum's prophecy brought great comfort and consolation to God's people since it predicts the fall of Nineveh—a ruthless, inhuman, wicked, and cruel city and the capital of the Assyrian Empire. In a day when cruelty was commonplace, cuneiform inscriptions found at Nineveh record atrocities that caused others of that day to pale into insignificance. Well-named, therefore, is Nahum, whose name means "comfort" or "consolation." His burden or message predicts the end of God's patience with Nineveh and the utter destruction of the city (1:14; 2:7–13; 3:11–19), which occurred in 612 B.C.

Nahum was a native of Elkosh, which Jerome states was located in Galilee. Its positive location, however, is uncertain. If from Galilee, then Nahum and Jonah (the only two prophets to deal with Nineveh) were from the same locale. This makes the pharisee's statement a lie: ". . . for out of Galilee arises no prophet" (John 7:52). Nahum's prophetic ministry can be dated from 660–655 B.C.

STUDY GUIDE OUTLINE TO NAHUM
1. The Jealousy of God *1*
2. The Judgment of God *2*
3. The Justice of God *3*

God's character, as holy, jealous, long-suffering, and yet as One who cannot tolerate sin forever and must punish wickedness, is one of the leading themes of the book.

Habakkuk

The prophet Habakkuk, whose name means "embrace," reverses the usual prophetic order. Instead of declaring God's message and thus standing between God and his people, he embraces God on behalf of the people and takes their perplexities to him, thus standing between the people and God. The thrust of his message is that the just shall live by faith (2:4). The ministry of Habakkuk is dated about 655–650 B.C.

Oppressed by their own leaders internally and subject to the punishment from God by the Babylonians externally, they ask three questions:

1. Why does God not answer prayer (1:1–4)?
2. Why does God use a wicked instrument, such as the Babylonians to punish his own people (1:5–11)?
3. Why do the wicked prosper and the righteous have such a difficult time (1:12–17)?

God states that to find the answer to these questions one must gain the proper spiritual perspective by drawing closer to God (2:1) and be patient (2:3). One will find that God answers prayer in his own way and in his best time. God also says that the Babylonians will ultimately be punished themselves and their judgment will be compounded because of their treatment of other nations (2:5–17). The final question is settled on spiritual, not material, principles. Only those who measure their prosperity in terms of God, not gold, are truly prosperous. The wicked appeal to their idols for help in time of need, but since there is no life in them, they cannot respond (2:18–19). But God always responds to and rewards those who live by faith (2:4).

The prophecy closes with a beautiful psalm of prayer, wherein the prophet cries out for revival (3:2) and confesses that, though God should take away all his material possessions, yet he "will rejoice in the LORD and . . . joy in the God of [his] salvation" (3:18).

STUDY GUIDE OUTLINE TO HABAKKUK

1. The Perplexities of the Prophet *1*
2. The Perspective of the Prophet *2*
3. The Praise of the Prophet *3*

A watchtower in fields near ancient Shechem. Habakkuk could not understand how God could use wicked Babylon to punish his people and climbed his watchtower to await an answer from God.

Zephaniah

Zephaniah means "the Lord hides or protects." Between the meaning of his name and the prediction that the great "day of the Lord" is imminent, there appears to be a connection, since the prophet urges the people to seek the Lord that they may "be hid in the day of the LORD's anger" (2:3). For a remnant shall be delivered in that day.

The prophet may have been of royal descent, since he traces his lineage to Hezekiah, who may be the king of that name. If so, he would have access to the good king Josiah, during whose reign he prophesied in the years 635–630 B.C. He would, therefore, be well informed on international affairs.

Zephaniah predicts a catastrophic invasion from the north, which may be that of the Scythians, which took place about 627 B.C., or that of the Babylonians under Nebuchadnezzar. From the scope of the nations involved and who will suffer devastation, the latter seems the one intended (2:4–15). Judah and Jerusalem (3:1–17) will also be crushed, as happened in 605–586 B.C.

From these events, the prophet leaps the centuries and predicts events of the end-time when God's wrath will be poured out upon the nations (3:8) and Israel will be restored (3:9–13) and experience kingdom blessings.

STUDY GUIDE OUTLINE TO ZEPHANIAH
1. The Consummateness of Judgment *1*
2. The Comprehensiveness of Judgment *2*
3. The Correctiveness of Judgment *3:1–8*
4. The Compassion in Judgment *3:9–20*

Haggai

Nothing definite can be known concerning the prophet Haggai. Some say that he was born in Jerusalem, while others claim that he was born in Babylon during the captivity. In any case, Haggai, whose name means "festal one," was an old man when he returned to Jerusalem after the exile (2:3).

Cyrus had granted a decree for the Jews to return to Jerusalem and rebuild the temple. Eagerly they undertook the work, but, meeting with hostility from the Samaritans and the delays caused by this, they lost their enthusiasm. Their financial problems, the failure of the crops, the difficulty of the task, and their dedication to the rebuilding and decorating of their own homes, brought the work on the temple to a halt. This continued for about eighteen years.

God's call came to Haggai, and he began his ministry by declaring that the unfavourable circumstances of the people were the result of disobedience. He urged the people to consider their ways and to get their spiritual priorities in order. Put God and his work first, he urges, and all other needs will be met. The people responded instantly. Some, however, again became discouraged when they realized that the beauty and glory of this temple was greatly overshadowed by that of Solomon. Haggai's command was, "Be strong!" This temple's glory will be greater for the desire of all nations (perhaps the Messiah) will come, and in the latter day he will dwell in it (2:4, 7, 9, 20–23). Haggai urges them to a solemn re-dedication of their lives to God; then God will take their former poverty away and bless them abundantly (2:11–19).

The prophet's four messages were delivered over a period of three months.

This great Menorah, or seven-branched lampstand, stands near the Israeli parliament. Zechariah had a vision of such a lampstand.

STUDY GUIDE OUTLINE TO HAGGAI

1. The Commitment of the Prophet and People *1:1–15*
2. The Comparison of the Two Temples *2:1–9*
3. The Cleansing of the People *2:10–19*
4. The Conquering of the Gentile Powers *2:20–23*

Zechariah

The name Zechariah means "the Lord remembers." This is the thrust of the prophecy. God remembered his people, and gave them opportunity to return from the exile. Only a remnant, however, returned and it is to this remnant that God declares his future dealings with them and with the nations of the world relating to them.

If the people are to have the blessings promised them, they need to put away the disobedient heart that characterized their fathers and brought them punishment. They are to learn the fundamental principle that obedience of the heart is better than the observance of rituals (1:4–6; 7:4–14).

The eight night visions which Zechariah recites signify that God

> **STUDY GUIDE OUTLINE TO ZECHARIAH**
>
> 1. The Calling of the People to Repentance *1:1–6*
> 2. The Comforting of the People Through the Visions *1:7–6:15*
> 3. The Coming to the People of a Messianic Deliverer *7:1–14:21*

is the sovereign ruler of heaven and earth, and that he will remember his people by crushing the nations that have persecuted them (1:7–2:13). God will cleanse his people through the expiatory work of the Messiah and will abundantly supply all their needs when restoration to the Lord takes place (3:1–4:14). Before this takes place, judgment will fall upon Israel and also upon the nations. Wickedness will then be removed and put in a permanent place (5:1–6:15). The Israelites will then look upon him whom they have pierced and by accepting him, their victory is assured against the nations. Thus they will live in peace and prosperity, when the Messiah's kingdom is established (8:1–14:21).

Many of the significant prophecies relating to Christ are found in this prophecy of Zechariah: he is called the Branch (3:8, 6:12), the King-Priest (6:13), the True Shepherd (11:4–11); his life is detailed under certain events—his triumphal entry (9.9), his betrayal (11:12), his death (12:10), his Second Coming (14:1–4), and his kingdom (14:16–21).

Malachi

Though the name Malachi means "my messenger," it would appear that it is used here as the name of the prophet. Nothing is known about him outside of this book. He ministered about one hundred years after Haggai and Zechariah, and the burden of his message was the coming judgment of the Lord upon the sins, wickedness, and infidelity of the priests and people.

Using the method of dialogue, a series of questions and answers characterize the sins committed:

1. The priests have profaned God's name and offered polluted bread and mutilated or diseased animals on the altar (1:6–2:9).

2. The people have also profaned God's holiness by marrying foreign wives, following divorce from their Jewish wives (2:10–16).

3. The people have wearied God by saying that everyone doing evil is good and God delights in them (2:17).

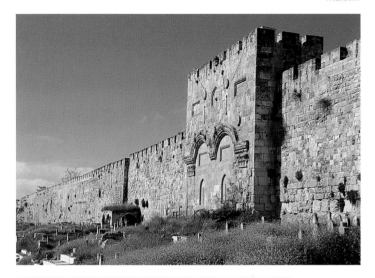

STUDY GUIDE OUTLINE TO MALACHI

1. The Charges Against Israel Pronounced *1*
2. The Covenant with Israel Violated *2*
3. The Coming to Israel Predicted *3–4*

The Golden Gate, Jerusalem. Tradition says that this gate will not open until the Messiah comes in glory.

4. The people have stolen from God by withholding the tithes (3:7–15) and thus God has withheld his blessing.

The warning now comes from the prophet that the Day of the Lord (4:1–6) is coming. The wicked will be punished, but those who fear God and were faithful shall be rewarded and enjoy eternal salvation. This speaks of both the first and second comings of Christ.

The closing admonition is to "remember the law of Moses" (4:5).

Between the Testaments

There is a period of some four centuries between the close of the Old Testament and the opening of the New. During this period, God's voice in divine revelation was still. No canonical books were written, though there were fifteen books produced which have been called the Apocrypha. Neither the Jews, nor Christ, nor the writers of the New Testament recognized the Apocrypha as canonical, though the Roman Catholic Church at the Council of Trent in A.D. 1546 declared them as canonical, with the exception of 1 & 2 Esdras and the Prayer of Manasseh.

In addition to the literary activity which resulted in the Apocrypha, there were other important developments which form the religious and cultural background of the New Testament.

Political History

1. The Persians governed the Jews from the time of the return from the Babylonian captivity to 332 B.C.

2. The Greeks brought the Jews under their domination with the conquest of the Persians by Alexander the Great. This opened up Palestine to the effects of Greek culture by Hellenization (332–301 B.C.).

3. The Ptolemaic, or Egyptian, period from 301–198 B.C. was a time when much Hellenization permeated Judaism and its lifestyle.

4. The Syrian period began with Antiochus III, who defeated the Egyptians in 198 B.C., and took control over Palestine. His successor, Antiochus IV, who was known as Epiphanes (the manifested one) but who was nicknamed Epimanes (the madman), sought to Hellenize the Jews completely, and endeavoured to destroy the religious practices of Judaism. He ordered pigs sacrificed on Jewish altars, and when a reprobate Jewish priest sought to do so, the Jews revolted and the Maccabean wars broke out. The fierce fighting zeal and military skill of the Maccabees finally drove the Syrians out of Palestine.

5. The Maccabean, or Hasmonean, period continued from 163 B.C. to 63 B.C., when Rome conquered Palestine.

6. The Roman period was a time when Rome ruled Palestine through either procurators, or rulers such as the Herodians. In 37 B.C., Herod the Great was placed as king and ruled until 4 B.C. It was during his reign that Christ was born and the slaughter of the infants at Bethlehem took place.

Orthodox Jews at Jerusalem's holy Western Wall, the main visible remnant of Herod's Temple.

Herod had three sons who followed him as rulers: Archelaus ruled over Jerusalem from 4 B.C. to A.D. 6, after which Judea was ruled by Roman procurators (from A.D. 41 to 44, however, King Herod Agrippa I ruled over Judea); Herod Antipas ruled over Galilee and Perea from 4 B.C. to A.D. 39; Philip ruled east and north of the Sea of Galilee from 4 B.C. to A.D. 34.

During the Roman period great power was concentrated in the hands of the high priest who, for all practical purposes, was the political leader of the Jews. The Roman period ended about A.D. 135.

Religious Developments

The religious developments during the four centuries between the Testaments saw the translation of the Septuagint (from about 250 to 150 B.C.), the rise of the Synagogue, and the establishment of the various religious sects: the Pharisees, Sadducees, and Essenes.

The **Pharisees** were the *legalists* of the day. They were devoted to the Law of Moses and sought to adapt and apply it to the varying conditions and experiences of life. They had a firm belief in the supernatural, angels, the immortality of the soul, the doctrines of the future life, future rewards and punishments, and the resurrection. When Jerusalem fell, the Pharisees kept Judaism alive because they were devoted to the Law of Moses; the fall of the city could destroy neither the Law nor the Pharisees and so both were preserved.

The **Sadducees** were the *rationalists* of the day. Their beliefs were governed by a sceptical attitude towards religion. They believed in the literal interpretation of the Law of Moses but did not allow it to have much effect on their lives. They denied the existence of angels, immortality, rewards, punishments, and the future life. They were materialistic and had an earthly outlook. Since they were connected primarily with the temple, its destruction brought about their gradual disappearance.

The **Essenes** were the *mystics* of their time. Some scholars have identified them with the Qumran community of the Dead Sea Scrolls, though there are some problems connected with such an identification. The Dead Sea Scrolls, however, are vitally important for our understanding of their type of communal life and teachings. A monastic community, the Essenes emphasized withdrawal from the world. They shared property in common and ate at a common table. They were vegetarians and their economy was based on labour in the fields. They abhorred filth in any form and their white apparel signified purity.

These parties made a significant impact on Judaism. The Sadducees were politically the most powerful party during New Testament times.

The moral conditions during these years were especially horrendous. Orgiastic practices in heathen worship, divorce, abortion, infanticide, prostitution, seduction, and adultery characterized the Gentile world. Despair was rampant and there was a desperate need for a Saviour.

The Greeks, the Romans, and the Jews

The Greeks, the Romans, and the Jews, with their important positions of leadership during these four centuries, made their own contributions to the world into which Christ came and through which Christianity spread.

The **Greeks**, the framers of classical expression and civilization, contributed in a most unusual way since it was into their language that the Old Testament was translated and was spread among the Jews through their synagogue worship. When God gave his revelation through the New Testament, it was written in the Greek language, for Greek was the language of commerce during this time.

The **Romans** left a legacy of law and order and a great highway system—some five main highways leading out from Rome

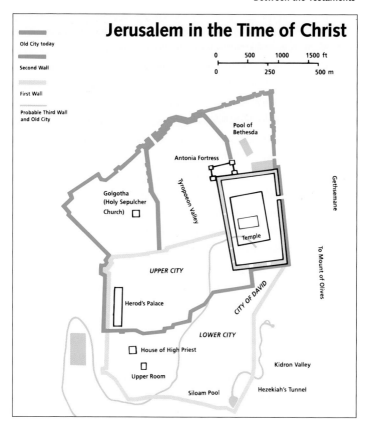

Jerusalem in the Time of Christ

Old City today

Second Wall

First Wall

Probable Third Wall
and Old City

0   500   1000   1500 ft
0   250   500 m

Pool of
Bethesda

Antonia Fortress

Tyropoeon Valley

Gethsemane

Golgotha
(Holy Sepulcher
Church)

Temple

To Mount of Olives

UPPER CITY

Herod's Palace

CITY OF DAVID

LOWER CITY

House of High Priest

Upper Room

Kidron Valley

Hezekiah's Tunnel

Siloam Pool

to the ends of the empire. Along these highways, the Gospel was taken to various parts of that great empire.

The **Jews** made a four-fold contribution: a belief in one God, the Scriptures in the common language of Greek, the synagogue as the place of public worship, and a strong faith in God. These all made a strong impact upon the heathen mind, and many became proselytes to Judaism.

During these centuries between the Testaments, in varied ways, God prepared the world for the coming of Christ, and as Paul stated: "But when the fullness of the time was come, God sent forth his Son, made of a woman, made under the law" (Galatians 4:4).

The New Testament

The divine revelation given in the New Testament is the record of God's redemptive activity as it culminates in the incarnation, crucifixion, and resurrection of Christ, and the spread of the gospel throughout the Roman Empire. It is contained in twenty-seven books, written under the superintendence of the Holy Spirit, by certain of the apostles or those in close relationship to the apostles.

These books relate the story of Christ's first coming, the origin of the church, the doctrinal and ethical teachings of the Christian faith, and the prophetic consummation of world history. These events may be summarized under four key words:

Revelation—The Gospels

A stretch of the Jordan river near the traditional site of Jesus' baptism by John the Baptist.

In the four gospels there is detailed a four-fold portrait of the birth, life, ministry, death, and resurrection of Christ. Christ is here revealed as the God-Man, who came to fulfil messianic prophecy and bring salvation to mankind. These four books are historical in nature.

Expansion—The Acts

After the death and resurrection of Christ, the apostles were told to wait for the coming of the Holy Spirit. The record of that event, and the origin of the church at that time, is found in this book. Subsequently, the preaching of the gospel, with the main emphasis on the resurrection of Christ, was rapidly taken by the apostles throughout the then-known world. So dynamic was this new faith that the apostles were named the men who turned the world upside down. In Acts, the church is seen on the move.

The view from the top of the great theatre at Ephesus where a riot was provoked during the apostle Paul's visit.

Instruction—The Epistles

Since the gospel must not only be preached but preserved, it was necessary to give instruction concerning its doctrinal and ethical content. This was the task of the letters written by various apostles either to local churches or individuals.

In the category of the doctrinal or church letters, the following books are found: Romans, 1 and 2 Corinthians, Galatians, Ephesians, Philippians, Colossians, 1 and 2 Thessalonians, Hebrews, James, 1 and 2 Peter, Jude and 1 John.

In addition, there are six letters written to individuals: 1 and 2 Timothy, Titus, Philemon, 2 and 3 John. These books deal with such subjects as sin, condemnation, salvation, justification, sanctification, the second coming, church problems such as doctrinal errors, the ethical conduct of the believer in relationship to the state, issues of domestic life, and leadership in the local church.

Trajan's Arch, Rome, commemorates the destruction of Jerusalem by the Romans in A.D. 70. The Roman soldiers are carrying off the seven-branched lampstand.

Consummation—The Book of Revelation

Alongside of this programme of instruction must go God's programme for the direction of history towards its final consummation. This prophetic programme is laid down in the book of Revelation. In it, God's plans for the church, the Jews, and the world are revealed as now working towards their completion. This book gives God's ending to the story of human civilization. It is a triumphant conclusion, in which redeemed man is seen in glory, Christ is King over all of life, and all of creation, with the believer, is freed from the bondage of corruption.

All of these books of the New Testament encompass the events and needs relating to the churches within a period of one century. As the inspired record of divine revelation, the precepts and principles of the New Testament govern the life of the believer both inside and outside the local church. With the Old Testament, they are the Scriptures which are "profitable for doctrine, for reproof, for correction, for instruction in righteousness: that the man of God may be perfect, thoroughly furnished unto all good works" (2 Timothy 3:16).

The Gospels

The Gospels give a four-fold portrait of the life and ministry of Christ. Many ask the question: "Why four gospels?" The answer is not difficult to find, since it is contained in the accounts themselves. Their contents clearly reveal that the four basic needs of mankind were met in the Saviour: political, governmental, intellectual, and spiritual.

These needs were exemplified in the basic characteristic needs of the people of that day:

1. The Jews desired a king: Matthew, therefore, presents Jesus as the *King*.

2. The Romans were vitally interested in good government, and in one who could accomplish great deeds: Mark presents Jesus as the worker of deeds and miracles, as the *Servant*.

3. The Greeks sought wisdom, knowledge, and understanding: in Luke's gospel is seen the scholarly and accurate presentation of Jesus as the Wisdom of God incarnate, the Submissive

Christian pilgrims gather at the entrance of the Garden Tomb, Jerusalem, a poignant reminder of Jesus' burial place.

One—God in human form as the *Man*.

4. The world at large needed a satisfying and sufficient Saviour, who could meet its spiritual needs: John presents Jesus as God indeed. In this One, who is Deity, the world finds the satisfying and sufficient Saviour, Christ as *God*.

Corresponding to this four-fold picture, which produced a full-orbed, unique, and unified view of Christ, the God-Man, there is also a relationship shown between the prophecies of the Old Testament concerning Christ and their fulfilment in his coming. In two Old Testament prophecies, the promised Messiah is revealed as the longed for *King* of the Jews (Jeremiah 23:5; Zechariah 9:9). In Matthew 27:37, Christ is presented as "Jesus the King of the Jews." For the concept of Christ as *Servant*, two prophetic references are seen in Isaiah 42:1 and Zechariah 3:8. Mark shows their fulfilment in Mark 10:45: "For even the Son of man came not to be ministered unto, but to minister, and to give his life a ransom for many." Prophesying concerning the humanity of the Messiah, Zechariah proclaims: "Behold the man whose name is The Branch; and he shall grow up out of his place, and he shall build the temple of the Lᴏʀᴅ" (6:12). Luke, who presents Christ as the *Man* uses an Old Testament title for the Messiah, portraying Christ's humanity: "For the Son of man is come to seek and to save that which was lost" (19.10). John, presenting Christ as truly *God* because of the miracles he wrought, writes: "And many other signs truly did Jesus . . . that ye might believe that Jesus is the Christ, the Son of God; and that believing you might have life through his name" (20:30–31). The prophetic promise of the Messiah's deity is given in Isaiah 40:9.

Though there is a four-fold picture, with a distinctive emphasis and destination for each gospel, given in the four gospels, yet three of them—Matthew, Mark, and Luke—are strikingly similar in subject matter and literary expression. Thus, the name Synoptic (presenting a similar point of view) gospels is given to these gospels. In seeking to explain both the similarities and differences (for these also exist), scholars have postulated a number of theories by which they attempt to solve what they call the "synoptic problem." That there were both written and oral sources available to the writers of the gospels (some were eyewitnesses to some of the events) is probable. It must be kept in mind, however, that any theory must not neglect the agency of the Holy Spirit, who superintended, guided, and controlled the revelation to and work of the writers, so that the product is the inspired record of the words of God in the language, style, and personality of the gospel writer.

Political Background in New Testament Times

Roman Emperors	Herodian Rulers	Procurators
Caesar Augustus 27 B.C.–A.D. 14	**Herod the Great 37–4 B.C.** King of Jews, great builder, Hellenizer.	
	Archelaus 4 B.C.–A.D. 6 Son of Herod, ethnarch of Judea, cruel.	
Birth of Jesus, boyhood at Nazareth	**Herod Antipas 4 B.C.–A.D.39** Tetrarch of Galilee and Perea. Killed John the Baptist.	
	Philip 4 B.C.–A.D. 34 Tetrarch of Iturea and Trachonitis.	
Tiberius Caesar 14–37 Public ministry, death, resurrection of Jesus		**Pontius Pilate** was Procurator of Judea and Palestine 26–36
Caligula 37–41 Growth of church, conversion of Paul	**Herod Agrippa I 37–44** Ruled tetrarchy of Philip, Judea, Perea, and Galilee (41–44)	
Claudius 41–54 Early missionary labours of Paul		
	Herod Agrippa II 50–100 Ruled former tetrarchy of Philip and Lysanias and parts of Galilee and Perea	
Nero 54–68 Paul's later labours; martyrdom at Rome		
Galba, Otho, Vitellius 68–69 Jewish Roman war in Palestine		
Vespasian 69–79 Fall and destruction of Jerusalem and the Jewish state; Jews scattered		
Titus 79–81		
Domitian 81–96 John's probable exile to Patmos; the book of Revelation		

Matthew

The gospel of Matthew has been assigned in authorship to Matthew, the tax-gatherer. While many critical scholars deny his authorship, they do so primarily on the basis of certain theories, brought forth to try to solve the synoptic problem. But to deny Matthew's authorship is to fail to give adequate credence to the unanimous tradition of the early church and to the obvious fact that Matthew was well qualified, as a tax-collector, to write it. He shows in the gospel an avid interest in numbers, money, and statistical enumerations such as the three-fold breakdown into fourteen generations each of Christ's genealogy, the ten thousand talents, and the talents to be invested (Matthew 1:17; 18:24; 25:15).

Also, Papias, an early church father, made the statement: "Matthew wrote the words in the Hebrew dialect. . . ." By this statement, he was probably not referring to an earlier gospel of Matthew in Aramaic but to the discourses of Jesus which he recorded in Aramaic and which he used as a basis to write his gospel in Greek. Thus, there is no adequate reason to reject Matthew's authorship.

There is agreement among most scholars that the gospel was written prior to the destruction of Jerusalem in A.D. 70. In one of Christ's discourses (Matthew 24:2), Matthew writes in terms that imply that the temple is still standing. This gospel was written, therefore, between A.D. 50 and A.D. 70.

The purpose of this gospel is to reveal Jesus as the legal heir to the throne of David. He is the son of David, the King of the Jews. To fulfil his purpose, Matthew presents three prominent facts concerning Christ:

1. His genealogy in which it is shown that he comes from the royal line of Judah (1:1–17).

2. His place of birth as Bethlehem of Judea, the royal city of David (2:1–2).

3. His ministry, and yet ultimate rejection, as King (21:9–11; 23:37–39).

4. His relationship to the promise to Abraham—including the central position of the Jew relative to its full provision to all people (1:2, 5; 12:18, 21; 28:18–20).

In presenting Christ, and in demonstrating his rightful claims to the rulership over the Jews as King, Matthew makes much of the idea of the kingdom. He uses, distinctively from the other gospels, the term "kingdom of heaven."

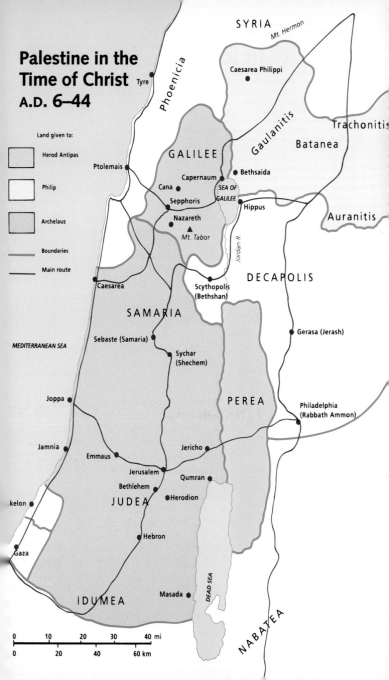

Palestine in the Time of Christ
A.D. 6–44

SYRIA

Mt. Hermon

Tyre

Caesarea Philippi

Phoenicia

Land given to:

Herod Antipas

Philip

Archelaus

Boundaries

Main route

Gaulanitis

Trachonitis

Batanea

GALILEE

Ptolemais

Capernaum

Bethsaida

Cana

SEA OF GALILEE

Sepphoris

Hippus

Auranitis

Nazareth

Mt. Tabor

Jordan R.

DECAPOLIS

Caesarea

Scythopolis (Bethshan)

SAMARIA

Gerasa (Jerash)

MEDITERRANEAN SEA

Sebaste (Samaria)

Sychar (Shechem)

Joppa

PEREA

Jamnia

Philadelphia (Rabbath Ammon)

Emmaus

Jericho

Jerusalem

Bethlehem

Qumran

kelon

Herodion

JUDEA

Gaza

Hebron

DEAD SEA

IDUMEA

Masada

NABATEA

| 0 | 10 | 20 | 30 | 40 mi |
| 0 | 20 | 40 | 60 km |

STUDY GUIDE OUTLINE TO MATTHEW

Christ as King
1. The Credentials of the King *1:1–4:11*
2. The Criteria of the Kingdom *4:12–7:29*
3. The Certification of the King *8:1–11:1*
4. The Content of the King's Teaching by Parables
     11:2–13:53
5. The Crisis of the King *13:54–26:2*
6. The Crucifixion of the King *26:3–28:20*

Distinctive features of Matthew, not found in the other gospels, include: the vision of Joseph (1:18–25), the visit of the wise men (2:1–12), the flight into Egypt (2:13–15), the slaughter of the infants (2:16–18), the death of Judas (27:3–5), the dream of Pilate's wife (27:9), the bribery of the guards (28:12–15), and the Great Commission (28:18–20).

Mark

Though Mark was not an apostle, he was in close association with Peter (1 Peter 5:13), and as the son of Mary, whose home in Jerusalem was a hub of activity in the early church (Acts 12:12), he had a living acquaintance with the trials and triumphs of the first Christians. There is reason, therefore, to believe that not only did he record eyewitness accounts of Christ's ministry given to him by Peter, but he may have witnessed some of the events himself. Mark is possibly the young man who fled naked from the garden (14:51–52). He is usually indicated as the John Mark of Acts 12:12, 25; 15:37. Also, he was related to Barnabas (Acts 15:36–39; Colossians 4:10). Later, he became closely associated with Paul, having evidently vindicated himself (2 Timothy 4:11).

Along with this internal evidence that Mark could have written this gospel, goes the external evidence which is very strong for Marcan authorship. Papias indicates that Mark was Peter's interpreter in this gospel. Justin Martyr calls this gospel the "memoirs of him," that is, Peter; and Irenaeus, having stated that Peter and Paul went to Rome, then adds that Mark, after their death, as the disciple and interpreter of Peter, wrote down what Peter had preached (compare references to Peter in Mark 1:36; 11:21; 13:3).

From this internal and external evidence, the conclusion can be drawn that Mark was the author of this gospel, and the date

STUDY GUIDE OUTLINE TO MARK

Christ as Servant
1. In Sonship *1:1–13*
2. In Service *1:14–13:37*
3. In Sacrifice *14:1–15:47*
4. In Supernatural Triumph *16:1–20*

Capernaum
•

for its writing can also be ascertained. Since neither Peter nor Paul reached Rome before Nero's persecution in A.D. 64, and since Mark does not say anything about the destruction of Jerusalem in A.D. 70, it appears to have been written between A.D. 65–70, with A.D. 67 as the probable date.

The purpose of Mark's gospel is to show that the Saviour is a man of action. The active words "immediately" and "straightway" are used frequently by Mark in recording the movements and works of Christ (1:10, 12, 18, 20, 21, 29; 5:13, 6:45, 8:10 etc.). To Mark, the Saviour is the Servant, and as he writes to the Romans, he explains Jewish customs and terms (5:41; 7:2–4, 11, 34). Additionally, the latinisms used by Mark would indicate it was written for the Romans.

Distinctive features of this gospel are minimal: he does not directly cite any Old Testament prophecies, he omits the genealogy of Christ, he places much emphasis upon the miracles (to indicate that Christ was a performer of deeds), and he gives interesting sidelights on those associated with Christ.

Christian pilgrims contemplate the Sea of Galilee from the slopes of the Mount of Beatitudes.

Luke

The gospel of Luke has been called by scholars the most literary of the gospels and the one gospel that approaches most nearly a biography of Christ. It is also the earlier of the two documents to come from the pen of Luke, the other being the book of Acts. Usually the two books are linked together in discussions of authorship, since they both have quite similar prefaces addressed to Theophilus ("Lover of God"). In this gospel preface, Luke sets as his goal that Theophilus "mightest know the certainty of those things, wherein thou hast been instructed" (1:4). And then, in the Acts, the story is carried on further in the expansion of the church as it continues that which "Jesus began both to do and teach, until the day in which he was taken up, after that he through the Holy Ghost had given commandments unto the apostles whom he had chosen" (Acts 1:1–2).

Though some scholars today question Luke's authorship, yet the internal and external evidence is so strong that it is nigh to impossible to deny this gospel to Lucan authorship.

Luke was called by Paul "the beloved physician" (Colossians 4:14) and the medical terms, as well as the interest of the writer in disease and sickness, strongly suggest a physician, such as Luke, as the author. Other internal evidence supports this: the same type of dedication, literary style, and vocabulary indicate that the author of Acts is the author of this gospel; the "we" sections of Acts (16:10–17; 20:5–21; 18; 27:1–28:16) show that the author was an associate of Paul on his missionary journeys, hence the one qualified to write these sections, as well as the rest of Acts. Along with this evidence goes the external evidence that the early church (by the middle of the second century) universally accepted this gospel as the work of Luke. It has been dated as to its writing between A.D. 58–60.

The Three-Fold Purpose of Luke's Gospel

1. To strengthen and confirm Theophilus in the Christian faith.

2. To show that Christ, submitting himself to the will of God in becoming man, is the perfect Man and the universal Saviour, who is able to save any who comes to him in faith, for "the Son of man is come to seek and to save that which was lost" (19:10).

3. To show the theme of redemption with Christ as our Redeemer (23:8; 24:21).

Parables of Jesus

	Matthew	Mark	Luke
New cloth on an old garment	9:16	2:21	5:36
New wine in old wineskins	9:17	2:22	5:37–38
Houses on rock and on sand	7:24–27		6:47–49
The two debtors			7:41–43
The sower and the soil	11:3–8	4:3–8	8:5–8
Lamp under a bushel	5:14–15	4:21–22	8:16; 11:33
The good Samaritan			10:30–37
The persistent friend			11:5–8
The rich fool			12:16–21
Servants watching for their master			12:35–40
The faithful steward			12:42–48
A fig tree without figs			11:6–9
The mustard seed	13:31–32	4:30–32	13:18–19
Leaven	13:33		13:20–21
Places of honour			14:7–14
The great banquet & reluctant guests			14:16–24
Counting the cost			14:28–33
The lost sheep	18:12–13		15:4–6
The lost coin			15:8–10
The prodigal son			15:11–32
The dishonest manager			16:1–8
The rich man and Lazarus			16:19–31
Servants and their duty			17:7–10
The unjust judge & the persistent widow			18:2–5
The Pharisee & the tax collector			18:10–14
Talents (or pounds)	25:14–30		19:12–27
The wicked tenants	21:33–41	12:1–9	20:9–16
Leaves on the fig trees	24:32–33	13:28–29	21:29–31
Return of the house-owner		13:34–36	
The growing seed		4:26–29	
Tares	13:24–30		
The hidden treasure	13:44		
Pearl of great value	13:45–46		
The fisherman's net	13:47–48		
The unforgiving debtor	18:23–34		
Labourers in the vineyard	20:1–16		
The two sons	21:28–31		
The wedding banquet	22:2–14		
Ten virgins	25:1–13		
The sheep and the goats	25:31–36		

Tradition has it that Jesus was born on this spot in Bethlehem, David's city.

STUDY GUIDE OUTLINE TO LUKE

Christ as the Perfect Man
1. In Preparation *1:1–4:15*
2. In Proclamation *4:16–9:62*
3. In Preaching Parables *10:1–18:30*
4. In Passion *18:31–24:53*

Features Distinctive to Luke

1. The genealogy of Christ, stressing his possession of all nations and position as the Saviour of all who trust in him among all peoples.

2. The story of the presentation of Christ in the temple (2:21–28); the preservation of the hymns inspired by the Holy Spirit (such as the songs of the angels, Mary, Elizabeth, and Zacharias).

3. The emphasis on the doctrine of the Holy Spirit (1:15, 35, 41, 67; 2:25, 26; 3:22; 4:1, 14, 18; 10:21; 24:49).

4. The teaching on prayer, praise, and thanksgiving (11:5–13; 18:1–8; 21:36, etc.).

5. The parabolic teaching on the sinful woman (7:36), the rich man and Lazarus (16:19–31), and the healing of the ten lepers (17:12–19).

6. The unique place given to women (for instance, the description of Mary and the other women at the cross 23:55–56; 24:1–11).

7. The strong emphasis upon children, so unusual for that particular time (7:12; 9:38).

8. The great stress upon the economic contrast between the rich and the poor (12:13–21).

9. The record of the whole Perean campaign of Christ (9:51–18:14).

John

The gospel of John is most unusual and differs radically from the other three gospels in its presentation of Christ's life and ministry. Rather than going into detail concerning Christ's life, it presents him instead in his personal relationships with men and women. John also confines himself to the mention of just seven miracles, which he calls signs. This gospel does not follow any chronological structure, and departs widely from the structure of the Synoptic gospels. Its style of writing is simple, but behind the style lies a profundity of thought that can never be fully fathomed. An example of this profundity is found in John's introduction of Jesus as the Logos (word or reason), a philosophical term in use in that day, especially by Philo. John empties the word of its philosophic trappings and applies it to Christ as the One who is eternal, the tangible revelation of God, and the Incarnate Son of God (1:1–18).

Who Wrote the Gospel of John?

The evidence, both internal and external, points to John, the one "whom Jesus loved" (13:23–25), as the one who "wrote these things" (21:24). The external evidence in the early church confirms the universal tradition that John wrote this gospel. Irenaeus stated that John, the Lord's disciple and the one, at the Last Supper, who leaned on Jesus' breast, wrote a gospel while residing in Ephesus. In this testimony there is a lineal descent from Irenaeus, who was a disciple of Polycarp, who in turn, was a disciple of John. Polycarp recited frequently the sayings of John the apostle; therefore, the testimony of Irenaeus bears the weight of Polycarp's witness.

Internal evidence shows that the author was a Palestinian Jew. He was well acquainted with Jewish feasts (2:13, 23; 5:1; 6:4; 7:37; 10:22; 13:1; 18:28) and Jewish customs (2:1–10; 3:25; 4:27; 11:38, 44, 53; 19:31, 40); he was very familiar with Palestinian geography (2:12–16; 3:23; 4:11, 20; 5:2; 8:20; 9:7; 10:22; 11:1, 18, 54; 18:1; 19:17); he was well known to the high priest (18:15); he was an eyewitness to the Lord's life and knew him intimately (1:14; 2:24; 4:1–3; 6:15; 11:33; 13:1, 21; 18:4; 19:35; 21:24); and he stresses the importance of belief (cognates of which occur about one hundred times in this gospel). Such an individual answers all the qualifications needed to write such a gospel and, among the disciples, John best fits as the author.

The so-called discovery by Eusebius of two Johns at Ephesus—John the Apostle and John the Presbyter—has led some recent

Ephesus

•

Mediterranean Sea

STUDY GUIDE OUTLINE TO JOHN
Christ as Fully God

1. In Revelation of the Son *1–4*
2. In Reaction towards the Son *5–6*
3. In Rebellion against the Son *7–12*
4. In Reclusion by the Son *13–17*
5. In Rejection of the Son *18–19*
6. In Resurrection of the Son *20*
7. In Responsibility for the Son *21*

critics to postulate that John the Presbyter was the author. This statement of Eusebius has been shown to have been misinterpreted, and both Johns refer to the same individual—John the Apostle, who was also John the Presbyter, or Elder (2 John 1; 3 John 1).

Tradition states that John the Apostle was the pastor of the church at Ephesus, and that Jesus' mother, Mary, was a member there. It also states that John died and was buried in Ephesus. Also, at the entreaties of his fellow disciples and bishops, according to the Muratorian Canon, John wrote his gospel as the last of the gospels. As a result of the testimonies of the early church fathers and others, as well as the absence of any reference to the destruction of Jerusalem, the writing of this gospel must be dated a number of years after A.D. 70. There is a consensus among scholars that it was written between A.D. 85 and 90.

The purpose of this gospel is clearly stated by John (20:30–31). He depicts Christ as truly God and, in order to convince men of this, John was divinely led to choose certain significant signs and wonders that would accomplish this purpose.

Features in John Not Common to the Other Gospels

1. He does not dwell on the parabolic method of teaching, for he mentions no parables.

2. He records four Passovers, while the other gospels only mention one.

3. He mentions a number of events not recorded in the other gospels, such as the miracle at Cana, the impotent man at Bethesda, the woman at the well, the raising of Lazarus, the high priestly prayer of John 17, the early Judean ministry of Christ, and the story of the adulterous woman.

4. He presents the great claims of Christ to answer the spiritual needs of everyone: he is the Bread of Life (6:35), the Light of the World (8:12; 9:5), the Good Shepherd (10:7, 11, 14), the

Miracles of Jesus

Miracle	Matthew	Mark	Luke	John
Jesus passes through angry crowd			4:28–30	
Demon-possessed man cured		1:23–26	4:33–35	
Peter's mother-in-law healed	8:14–15	1:30–31	4:38–39	
Catch of fish			5:1–11	
Leper healed	8:2–3	1:40–42	5:12–13	
Paralyzed man healed	9:2–7	2:3–12	5:18–25	
Man's withered hand healed	12:10–13	3:1–5	6:6–10	
Centurion's servant healed	8:5–13		7:1–10	
Widow's son raised from the dead			7:11–15	
Calming of the storm	8:23–27	4:37–41	8:22–25	
Demon-possessed man healed	8:28–34	5:1–15	8:27–35	
Jairus' daughter raised from dead	9:18–25	5:25–42	8:41–56	
Haemorrhaging woman healed	9:20–22	5:25–29	8:43–48	
Five thousand people fed	14:15–21	6:35–44	9:12–17	6:5–13
Demon-possessed boy healed	17:14–18	9:17–29	9:38–43	
Blind, dumb, and possessed man healed	12:22		11:14	
Woman with a bent back healed			13:11–13	
Man with dropsy healed			14:1–4	
Ten lepers healed			17:11–19	
Bartimaeus and blind man healed	20:29–34	10:46–52	18:35–43	
Malchus' ear healed			22:50–51	
Two blind men healed	9:27–31			
Dumb and possessed man healed	9:32–33			
Money found in fish's mouth	17:24–27			
Deaf and dumb man healed		7:31–37		
Blind man healed		8:22–26		
Water turned into wine				2:1–11
Nobleman's son healed of fever				4:46–54
Invalid at Pool of Bethesda healed				5:1–9
Man born blind is healed				9:1–41
Lazarus raised from the dead				11:1–44
Second catch of fish				21:1–11
Walking on water	14:25	6:48–51		6:19–21
Canaanite woman's daughter healed	15:21–28	7:24–30		
Four thousand people fed	15:32–38	8:1–9		
Fig tree withers	21:18–22	11:12–26		

Resurrection (11:25), and the Vine (15:1).

5. He omits certain significant events such as the Sermon on the Mount, the Transfiguration, and the agony in Gethsemane.

Acts

Various titles have been given to this book. It has been called the book of Acts, the Acts of the Apostles, and, more properly, the Acts of the Holy Spirit. This latter title details the secret for the success of the Christian expansion of the Christian faith. The power of the Holy Spirit, which Christ instructed his disciples to wait for, is that which motivated and energized the early preachers of the gospel. His power brought conviction upon sin-sick Jewish hearts and later Gentile lives, and many were added to the faith as the gospel surged across the Roman Empire.

The question of the authorship of this book is basically settled when one has established the authorship of Luke's gospel. Both of these books go together; Acts is the second volume of Luke's record of what Jesus "began to do and to teach" as it relates to his post-ascension ministry from heaven through his apostles. The internal and external evidence plus the historical accuracy of the book strongly argue for the Lucan authorship. The book, therefore, was written by Luke, and, since Paul probably arrived in Rome about A.D. 59, and had probably been in Rome for about two years when the book of Acts closed, the date of the book's writing can be placed at A.D. 61.

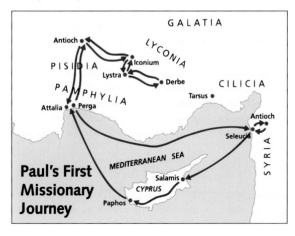

Paul's First Missionary Journey

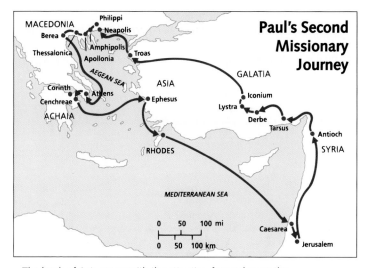

Paul's Second Missionary Journey

The book of Acts opens with the attention focused upon the post-resurrection teaching ministry of Christ for forty days with the apostles. Christ instructed them on "the things pertaining to the kingdom of God" (1:3) and commanded them to "wait for the promise of the Father" (1:4), which meant that they would "be baptized with the Holy Ghost not many days hence" (1:5). While we do not know what Christ taught his disciples concerning the kingdom, yet we do know what task he assigned them to perform: they were "to be witnesses unto me both in Jerusalem, and all Judea, and in Samaria, and unto the uttermost part of the earth" (1:8).

The purpose, therefore, of the book of Acts is to record the early events associated with this task, as the apostles carried it out under the empowerment of the Holy Spirit. The message which was preached in the fulfilment of the task was that the blood of Christ alone brings about the remission of sins (4:12), and that this message was vindicated by God when he raised Christ from the dead (1:3; 2:24, 27; 3:15; 4:10; 10:40; 17:31). For those who reject this message of life eternal, a day of judgment has been appointed for them, as Paul reminds his hearers (17:30–31). This day of judgment has been also guaranteed by Christ's resurrection from the dead.

Certain pivotal points in fulfilling this task are underscored in the book: the ascension of Christ (1:9–11), granting the disciples the *authority* for the task; the baptism of the Holy Spirit

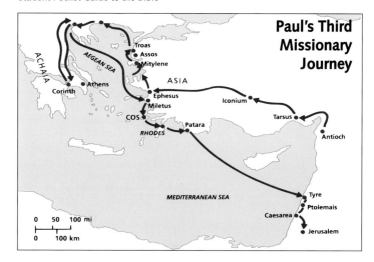

Paul's Third Missionary Journey

STUDY GUIDE OUTLINE TO ACTS

The person and work of the Holy Spirit

1. The Decision to Await His Coming to Establish the Church *1*
2. The Descent to Originate the Church *2:1–4*
3. The Dynamic to Empower the Church *2:5–4:37*
4. The Discipline to Purify the Church *5:1–42*
5. The Direction to Guide the Church *6:1–28:31*
   a. *In Administration 6:1–15*
   b. *In Persecution 7:1–8:3*
   c. *In Evangelism 8:4–14:28*
   d. *In Conference 15:1–29*
   e. *In Expansion 15:30–28:31*

(2:1–4), granting them the *power* for the task as they carried it on through the instrument of the church; the disciplinary action of Peter (5:1–11), demonstrating the church's *right* to keep itself pure as the task was carried out; the origin of deacons (6:1–8), granting to the disciples *the official helpers* in performing the task; the martyrdom of Stephen (7:1–60) granting them the *vision* and *incentive* to expand the areas in which the task should be pursued; the conversion of Paul (9:1–15) granting them *the leader* to fulfil the task among the Gentiles; and the Council at Jerusalem (15:1–29), granting them *the pure gospel of God's*

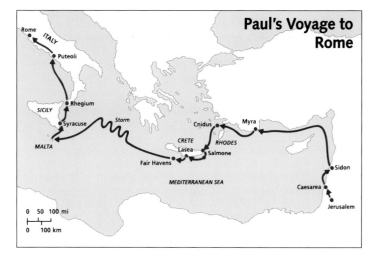

Paul's Voyage to Rome

grace as the only message needed to accomplish the task.

As the task of evangelization was carried out, the book of Acts records that God used certain outstanding personalities: Peter, chapters 1–5; Stephen, chapters 6–7; Philip, chapters 8–12; and Paul, chapters 13–28. The book closes with Paul "in his own hired house, and received all that came in unto him, preaching the kingdom of God, and teaching those things which concern the Lord Jesus Christ, with all confidence, no man forbidding him" (28:30–31).

Romans

If any letter of Paul can be named the greatest of all his letters, then that honour must fall to the book of Romans. It is the inspired systematic theology of the Christian faith. Some have said that every great revival in the Christian church began with the preaching of the book of Romans.

The tradition of the church has always considered Paul to be the author of this book, and it was only in recent times that any denial of his authorship was advanced. There are, however, no strong arguments that would deny the letter as Pauline. From Irenaeus on, the external evidence uniformly supports Paul's authorship; the internal evidence shows that the writer calls himself Paul (1:1), and other allusions to the writer (11:13; 15:15–20)

STUDY GUIDE OUTLINE TO ROMANS

1. The Reprobation of Humankind *1:1–3:20*
2. The Redemption of Humankind *3:21–8:39*
3. The Reconciliation of Israel *9:1–11:36*
4. The Responsibility of Believers *12:1–16:27*

show that only Paul could answer the descriptions.

The reason for writing this letter is given by Paul himself (1:10–13); he wanted to visit the believers at the church in Rome, but so far had been prevented by various circumstances. The date of its writing is later than 2 Corinthians because Paul, according to Romans 15:25, is about to depart for Jerusalem and he had written 2 Corinthians while in Macedonia earlier. Now he is in Corinth, where he stayed three months (Acts 20:2–3) and from which he writes this Roman letter in A.D. 56.

The purpose of this letter is to strengthen the believers in Rome in the great doctrines of the Christian faith. In all probability, the church at Rome was composed largely of Gentile believers, with perhaps some Jewish believers, though the Jewish believers were probably in the minority. These Gentile believers would need instruction not only in the doctrines of the faith (1–11) but also in the practical application of these doctrines to the everyday life of the believer (12–16).

After a rather lengthy introduction to the letter, the apostle gets down to those matters in which he feels the believers need instruction. To point up these matters, he utilizes four basic questions:

1. What is wrong with the world? (1:18–3:20)
2. How can the world be restored? (3:21–8:39)
3. How does Israel fit into this situation? (9:1–11:36)
4. How does the believer relate his faith to everyday life? (12:1–16:27)

As the apostle answers these questions, he presents the thrust of his teachings. The world, having turned its back on God, is under the curse of sin, and all the classes of humankind are sinners and under condemnation for their guilt:

1. The heathen world (1:18–32)
2. The moral person (2:1–16)
3. The religious person (2:17–29)

All are guilty and under condemnation, none can be justified by any merit, good works, or adherence to the law (3:19–20). The only way by which the world can be restored is through the redemptive work of Christ. To be restored to a right relationship

Part of the forum of ancient Rome.

to God, we can only be saved by God's grace in Christ and justified (declared righteous) by faith (3:21–5:21). And, in order to maintain a life of victory and righteous living in Christ (6:1–7:25), we must know what Christ has done for us (6:2–10), reckon that we have died to sin and the body of sin has been rendered inoperative (6:11), and then yield ourselves as instruments of righteousness (6:13), and yielding demanding obedience to the Word of God (6:17). Obedience daily to the Word brings progressive sanctification in Christ. This way of God in sanctification is contrasted to the human way (chapter 7), and the failure that entails. But the believer can never lose his salvation, however, because nothing can separate the believer from Christ (8:1–39).

Now the question facing the apostle is how this salvation relates to Israel. Have God's chosen people been abandoned in favour of the Gentiles? Paul's answer is a resounding, No! Israel has been judicially blinded for a time (11:7), but God will not forsake his people forever. He will remember his covenant with them; and the day will come when all Israel will be saved (11:25–36).

Paul comes at this time to the practical application of doctrinal truth. The believer should now yield completely to God and put his or her spiritual priorities in order:
1. Surrender to God (12:1–2)
2. Evaluate his or her own abilities properly (12:3–8)
3. Then lovingly serve others (12:9–21)

Following this, the believer must not neglect his or her responsibilities in relation to civic matters (chapter 13), to church matters (chapter 14), or to ministerial matters (chapter 15). With these admonitions, the apostle then closes his letter with an extended list of personal greetings (chapter 16).

Rome
●

1 Corinthians

Corinth
•

Mediterranean Sea

First Corinthians is unusual in the sense that it gives one a look into the heart of a local church, and the picture gained is what one would expect were we to look into any local church in any age. Local churches are made up of regenerated people (and some unregenerated ones), but even such people have their problems. This letter to the church in Corinth deals with such problems as divisions over which group is most prestigious, immorality, marital relations, Christian liberty, ministerial remuneration, conduct at the Lord's Supper, spiritual gifts, and the order of the resurrection. While these problems greatly disturbed the church, and they wrote to Paul to seek counsel in solving them, the apostle not only dealt with the problems but wrote a superb discourse on love, which, if applied daily in life, would eliminate most problems and bring peace and purity to the church.

The problems which vexed the church in Corinth were, perhaps, indigenous to the city. Corinth was a wealthy seaport, enjoying a luxurious commercial trade and populated by Romans, Greeks, and Jews. Moral standards were exceedingly loose, idolatry abounded, and vice was rampant. These, in themselves, could be the cause of many of the problems within the church. The difficulties of young believers in adjusting to the Christian life amidst the lax moral standards out of which they have just come, and the problems associated with eating meats offered to idols, all troubled them. Temptations to worldliness were powerful, and would account for the lapses from spiritual living.

The church in Corinth was founded by Paul after he left Athens and came to Corinth (Acts 18:1–18). Following his residence in Corinth, he went to Ephesus with Aquila and Priscilla. He later went to Palestine, and then returned to Syrian Antioch, and finally Ephesus. Paul wrote this letter, in all probability, towards

---

STUDY GUIDE OUTLINE TO 1 CORINTHIANS

1. Disorders in the Church *1:1–4:21*
2. Discipline in the Church *5:1–6:8*
3. Directions in Marital Relationships *6:9–7:40*
4. Demonism and Decorum in the Communion Service *8:1–11:34*
5. Diversity in Spiritual Gifts *12:1–14:40*
6. Death in the Light of the Resurrection of Christ *15:1–58*
7. Demands in the Gospel Work *16:1–24*

the end of his stay in Ephesus. The date would then be either A.D. 54 or 55.

The purpose of the letter is to enable the believers to understand their Christian responsibilities in relationship to the local church (1:1–4:21), to moral standards (5:1–6:20), to marital relationships (7:1–40), to food offered to idols (8:1–13), to conduct at the Lord's Supper (11:1–34), and to the use of spiritual gifts (12:1–31). Also the apostle lays down the need for the believer to be governed by the law of love, which is the greatest gift. The closing chapters give the believer the stabilizing hope of the resurrection (15:1–58).

Columns of the ancient Temple of Apollo, Corinth— a wealthy seaport, enjoying a luxurious commercial trade and populated by Romans, Greeks, and Jews.

2 Corinthians

Second Corinthians is an intensely personal letter and one that lays bare the soul of the apostle to the Corinthians. It is autobiographical and reveals the strong ties of love between the apostle and his converts. This letter is in response to a severe letter that Paul had in all probability written to the Corinthians, but has since been lost (though it is not the lost letter of 1 Corinthians 5:9) and which was written between 1 and 2 Corinthians.

The occasion for 2 Corinthians was the report of Titus to Paul when they met in Macedonia, and Titus had reported on the spiritual condition of the Corinthians. Titus stated that the majority of the Corinthians had repented of their opposition to Paul, and supported the gospel that he preached. A minority, however, still were hostile to Paul, and had evidently organized against

STUDY GUIDE OUTLINE TO 2 CORINTHIANS

1. The Apostle's Principles of Action *1–7*
2. The Apostle's Provision for the Poor Saints *8–9*
3. The Apostle's Polemic for His Ministry *10–13*

him under one judaizing preacher (10:7).

Paul now responds to the Corinthians in this, his possibly fourth, letter to the Corinthians—the other two (compare 1 Corinthians 5:9; 2 Corinthians 2:3–4, 9; 7:8–12) have been lost.

Paul commences this letter by stating that, contrary to the charges of the Judaizers, God had blessed his ministry because it was characterized by prayer, simplicity, and godly sincerity (1:11–2:17). Additionally, he states that the best accreditation for his apostolical authority lay in the Corinthians themselves—their salvation by God's grace through the simple gospel and their continuance in the faith validated his ministry (3:1–5:20).

He then turns to their stewardship in giving to God's work, and reminds them of their commitment to give generously to God's people. He states that stewardship is *grounded* in grace (8:1–7), is *governed by* the voluntariness of personal giving in love to Christ (8:8–12, 24; 9:2, 7), is *granted* to every Christian as a spiritual privilege (8:12–15), is to be in proportion to income (8:14; 9:7), and is *glorifying* to God, for it sends forth the gospel (9:13–14).

The apostle closes by vindicating his ministry against the Judaizers who oppose him. He shows that he is not worldly, as charged, but mighty through God (10:1–6); he is not weak and cowardly, though his bodily appearance leaves much to be desired (10:7–11); and that he is boasting only in the Lord (10:12–18). He also warns against false teachers (11:13–15) and states that his glorying is in the Lord, who has richly blessed his ministry (11:16–33; 12:1–13:4).

From the time of Polycarp on, the tradition of the church has been that Paul is the author of this letter, though some scholars have questioned its unity by saying that the letter to which Paul is replying is not lost, but is contained in chapters 10–13. This, however, does not appear to be true. This letter (2 Corinthians) was written by Paul from Macedonia shortly after 1 Corinthians and thus is dated between A.D. 54 and 55. The internal evidence also supports the Pauline authorship (2:13; 7:5–7; 8:1; 9:2–4). It is too personal to have been written by a forger.

Galatians

Along with the letters to the Romans and the two to the Corinthians, Galatians deals with the ever-recurring problem of the teaching of the Judaizers. The problem of the relationship of the law to the gospel, though solved by the Council of Jerusalem (Acts 15), and dealt with by Paul repeatedly, seems never to have been put to rest—not even at the present time.

The authorship of this letter has never really been strenuously contested. The external evidence from Clement of Rome onward has supported Pauline authorship, and the internal evidence has been equally powerful. There would be no purpose for any other writer to forge a letter that deals with the questions of circumcision and Paul's apostolic authority.

The destination of this letter, however, has been the subject of much debate. Did Paul write this letter to the Galatian churches in North Galatia, founded on his second and third missionary journeys? Or, did he write it to the churches in South Galatia, established on the first missionary journey (Acts 13:14–14:23)?

It would appear that the evidence supports the South Galatian view, since the churches of the important cities of Lystra, Derbe, Iconium, and Antioch in Pisidia are located there, and the Judaizing teachers would hardly bypass these important cities to go to the

Remains of the ancient aqueduct at Antioch in Pisidia, an early site of Paul's missionary activities.

STUDY GUIDE OUTLINE TO GALATIANS

1. Defence of Paul's Apostleship 1:1–9
2. Declaration of Paul's Authority 1:10–2:14
3. Delineation of Paul's Argument 2:15–6:18

remote regions of North Galatia. That Paul uses the term "Galatians" rather than the names of the cities does not militate against this view since the New Testament writers frequently used a territorial, rather than an ethnically distinctive, name for a city or district (see Acts 2:10; 18:2, 24; 20:4).

The next question is: Did Paul write this letter before the time of the Council of Jerusalem (Acts 15) or after the Council and about the same time as 1 and 2 Corinthians? The answer would seem to be that it was before the time of the Council, hence about A.D. 48/49. If it were afterwards, why did Paul not quote the Council's decision to the Galatians relative to the relationship of the law to the gospel (Acts 15:19–35)?

The purpose of Paul's writing to the Galatians is clear: the law of Moses, with its ceremonial demand for circumcision, is not to be added to the free gospel of the grace of God in salvation by faith alone in Christ. So deeply stirred was Paul by the reports that the Judaizers were misleading the Galatians by demanding that the law or good works be added to salvation by grace through faith alone, that he wrote the Galatians immediately by his own hand. He printed by hand the letters of each word because his eyesight was so poor (Galatians 6:11: "You see with what large letters I have written unto you with mine own hand").

Paul defends first of all his apostleship by showing that he received the gospel by revelation from Christ (1:12), and the apostles he visited in Jerusalem added nothing to it—he was their equal (1:15–2:21). Then he climaxes his argument on the gospel of God's free grace by faith alone by showing that the law has no place in relationship to saving a person by grace, for as the Holy Spirit was given by grace so also was salvation (3:1–9), that the law brings death and condemnation and not life and salvation (3:10–18), and finally, that the purpose of the law is to reveal that men and women are sinners, to lead them to Christ, and to magnify God's grace (3:19–29). He draws the letter to a close showing a contrast between Sarah (the free woman) and Hagar (the bond woman) and then admonishing the Galatians to walk in the fruit of the Spirit (5:1–6:18).

Ephesians

This letter to the Ephesians is one of the so-called prison letters of Paul, so named because they were written while Paul was serving his first prison term in Rome. This would place the writing of the letter about A.D. 61. According to Ephesians 6:21–22, Tychicus delivered this letter to the Ephesians. Since the words "at Ephesus" are not in many of the best Greek manuscripts, most scholars believe that the letter is a circular one, and was to be circulated among the various churches, such as Laodicea, in the area of Ephesus in Asia Minor.

The purpose of the letter is two-fold and thus accounts for the general, rather than specific, nature of the letter. It was written:

1. To reveal the mystery of the church (universal not local), which means that Jew and Gentile are members on an equal basis in one body (3:1–7).

2. To remind the believer to walk worthily in his daily life in harmony with his position in Christ "in the heavenlies" (1:3, 20; 2:6; 4:1–5:33; 6:12–20).

The apostle opens the letter by saying that our position in the heavenlies is by virtue of our sovereign election in Christ (1:4) and that we have been predestined unto the adoption of children (1:5) so as to be made conformable to the image of the Son, and have been sealed with the Holy Spirit of promise (1:13).

The single column in this photo is all of importance that remains of the once spectacular Temple of Diana, or Artemis, Ephesus.

STUDY GUIDE OUTLINE TO EPHESIANS

1. The Will of God *1:1–23*
2. The Work of God *2:1–3:21*
3. The Walk for God *4:1–6:9*
4. The Warfare for God *6:10–24*

Philippi
●

Aegean Sea

Available to the believer in his or her daily walk in Christ's body is the same great power of God by which he raised Christ from the dead (1:17–23).

Continuing his argument, Paul states the meaning of salvation as a gift of God's grace (2:1–9) alone through faith. And now it is the believer's responsibility to manifest his or her salvation before others (2:10–22).

In chapter 3, the apostle reveals the mystery of the church. In contrast to the Old Testament period, during which the Gentile could only be saved in relationship to God's chosen people, Israel, now the Gentile and the Jew have equal opportunity for salvation in Christ, and they dwell equally as one in Christ's body, the church (3:1–21).

Concluding his argument, Paul exhorts believers to walk worthily in daily conduct so that they may show forth the position which they have "in the heavenlies" with Christ. This is to be done as children of light (5:8) in every area of life: in marital relationships, in parental duties, and in work situations (5:22–6:10). The final exhortation is to put on the "whole armour of God" in order to fight against "principalities and powers" (6:11–24).

Philippians

Philippians is a tender and affectionate personal letter of Paul to a church which was very precious to him. He had deep ties of love to the members of this church; joy and delight characterized his thoughts as he remembered their generosity to the poor saints in Jerusalem and to him personally (4:10–19; compare Romans 15:25; 1 Corinthians 16:2; 2 Corinthians 8:1–4). As they were his joy, then they should also rejoice in the Lord, which is one of the main themes of this letter (1:4, 25, 26; 2:2, 16–18, 28, 33; 4:4, 10).

The church at Philippi, an important city in Macedonia and a Roman colony, was founded by Paul in response to a vision (Acts 16:9–40). Now, he writes this letter to this church (which was partly begun in a prison) from a prison in Rome. His purpose in

The impressive Library of Celsus, ancient Ephesus.

writing to the Philippians was manifold:

1. To express his thanksgiving to God for their love for him and their continuing progress in the Christian life (1:1–11).

2. To give them a report on his present circumstances (1:12–26).

3. To beseech them to have the same attitude as Christ in unity, humility, and obedience in service (1:27–2:18).

4. To send a note of commendation and explanation for sending Timothy and Epaphroditus (2:19–30).

5. To warn them against false teachers and to exhort them to walk worthily of Christ (3:1–21).

The Roman forum, ancient Philippi.

STUDY GUIDE OUTLINE TO PHILIPPIANS

1. Christ Our Provision *1*
2. Christ Our Pattern *2*
3. Christ Our Power *3*
4. Christ Our Peace *4*

6. To urge them to joyfulness, prayer, and the contemplation of all which is good and virtuous (4:4–9).

7. To thank them for their recent gift and previous generosities (4:10–20).

Both the external evidence in the tradition of the church (Clement of Rome, Polycarp, and others) and the internal evidence of literary style (historical events and personal expressions as seen in 1:1; 4:10–20) convincingly argue for Pauline authorship. Since Paul was in prison in Rome, the date of writing would be about A.D. 60–61.

Paul, interestingly enough, did not introduce himself as an apostle but as a servant of Christ (1:1). This reveals that the Philippians did not question Paul's apostleship and that Paul wanted to emphasize the concept of servanthood for himself and for the Philippians, as they both emulate Christ's servanthood (2:5–8). For the entrance to exaltation both for Christ and the believer is through suffering and service (2:17–30). Such exhortations show the intensely personal nature of this letter.

Colossians

Colossians, which is similar to Ephesians, was also written by Paul from his prison in Rome around A.D. 60–61. The evidences externally (from Ignatius onward) and internally (the writer calls himself Paul—1:1, 23; 4:18) are very powerful for authorship by Paul.

The letter was occasioned by the visit of Epaphras to Paul in prison at Rome. The visit's purpose was two-fold:

1. To encourage Paul by communicating the love of the Colossians for him.

2. To lay before Paul the need of the Colossian church for instruction and edification.

False teachers had come into that region, teaching a doctrine which combined the legalism of the law of Moses with an oriental mysticism and superstition (2:8–18).

This teaching was an early form of Gnosticism, a spurious form of higher knowledge which boasted ability to fathom the depths of spiritual mysteries. Gnostics taught, among other things, that there was a host of demi-gods, or spirit beings, in various

Colosse
•

Mediterranean Sea

Tombs on Rome's ancient Appian Way. The apostle Paul was probably executed in Rome.

STUDY GUIDE OUTLINE TO COLOSSIANS

Paul Exalts Christ as the Head of the Church

1. The Declarations of Paul *1:1–14*
2. The Dignity of Christ *1:15–29*
3. The Doctrines of the Church *2:1–34*
4. The Duties of the Christian *3:5–4:18*

gradations, one of whom was Christ. To reach Christ, one had to go through a series of intermediary and angelic beings. They asserted also, however, that there were other demi-gods even above Christ and between him and the invisible God.

Against a background of such false teaching, the reasons why Paul made certain strong statements can be understood. Against their claim that God did not dwell fully in Christ, Paul said: "For in him dwelleth all the fullness of the Godhead bodily" (2:9; 1:15, 18–19). Since Gnosticism considered matter as evil, for Paul to say God dwells bodily in Christ was an especially strong rebuke to them. In their teaching that Christ was an inferior being to God, for Paul to assert his equality with God and his superiority over other beings was an insult: "And ye are complete in him, which is the head of all principality and power . . ." (2:10–15). Paul also levels charges against the Judaizers and their legalism (2:11, 13, 14–23). Additionally, Paul's use of the words "knowledge," "wisdom," "spiritual understanding," and "powers of darkness" declares that in Christ alone is found true spiritual knowledge and understanding, rather than in the false teachings. Also in contrast to the charge that God could never be known, Paul contends that Christ is the fully expressed image of God, and he can be known and trusted for salvation. The apostle also reveals that, if there is to be the death of the body, then it is not to be accomplished in the ascetic, fleshly mortification demanded by false teachers but in the spiritual mortification of the members of the body. For the believer's new life is in the resurrected Christ, who gives us daily victory over fleshly desires and lusts (chapter 3).

1 & 2 Thessalonians

The two letters of Paul to the Thessalonian church are among the earliest of Paul's writings. During this early period, a most vital concern was that of the return of Christ. Many questions and problems were associated with this doctrine. To help the believers in Thessalonica, therefore, to understand more clearly this teaching of Christ's return was one of the reasons that Paul wrote these letters.

The historical background of the Thessalonian church is found in Acts 17:1–9. Paul arrived in this city from Philippi, where he had founded the first European church. Bearing in his body the marks of suffering for Christ, he came to this busy, wealthy, commercial seaport of Thessalonica. As was his custom, he went immediately to the synagogue, where he preached Christ to the Jews first, for the city had a flourishing community of Jewish families. There was also in this synagogue a group of Gentile proselytes.

To Paul's preaching came a two-fold reaction; an avid reception, especially by the proselytes and the heathen Gentiles; but among the Jews broke out a violent and bitter reaction which necessitated Paul's departure from the city. An aggressive and growing church, however, resulted (Acts 17:3–4).

Making his way from Thessalonica to Berea, then to Athens,

Thessalonica

Mediterranean Sea

Remains of a Roman dungeon in Philippi, Macedonia— probably the jail where Paul was imprisoned.

STUDY GUIDE OUTLINE TO 1 & 2 THESSALONIANS

1. Our Hope in Christ *1 Thessalonians*
  a. Spirituality of Believers *1*
  b. Sufferings of Believers *2*
  c. Sanctification of Believers *3*
  d. Second Coming for Believers *4*
2. Our Glorification in Christ *2 Thessalonians*
  a. Comfort for Believers in Persecution *1*
  b. Counsel for Believers in Prophecy *2:1–12*
  c. Commands for Believers in Practical Living *2:13–3:18*

and finally Corinth, Paul awaited with anxiety the coming of Timothy and Silas with a report on the work at Thessalonica. This report is reflected in 1 Thessalonians 3:6–8.

The glad tidings brought by Timothy and Silas are undoubtedly the occasion for writing the letters to the Thessalonian church. The writer of both these letters calls himself Paul (1 Thessalonians 1:1; 2:18; 2 Thessalonians 1:1; 3:17), and along with the external evidence, which is quite adequate, there is no need to deny the Pauline authorship. The date for the writing of both these letters from Corinth was A.D. 50–51. Interestingly, in his letter to the Philippians and his two letters to the Thessalonians, Paul does not call himself "an apostle"; the probable reason for this is the mutually loving relationship between these churches and Paul.

The first epistle discusses in broad outline two vital subjects which concerned the churches: the apostle's encouragement to the church because of the various sufferings and persecutions it was experiencing and the doctrine of the second coming of Christ as it relates to faith and life.

A few months after the reception of Paul's first letter, the Thessalonians received another letter to supplement the instructions of the first. This letter was to assure the Thessalonians that they were not going through the time called the wrath of God. The Day of the Lord will not come until the apostasy manifests itself and the "man of lawlessness" has been revealed (2:2–10). They are, therefore, to live godly in the light of the imminence of the Lord's return, and those who had ceased to work because they were awaiting Christ's early return were to return to work, or not be supported by others (3:6–15). They had been informed already of the signs which would herald the Day of the Lord.

The Pastoral Letters

Aegean Sea

CRETE

The letters of 1 and 2 Timothy and Titus come from the final days of the apostle's life. The final picture in Acts speaks of Paul's being in prison at Rome. Many scholars believe that Paul was released from this imprisonment, as the allusions to this in 2 Timothy 4:16–17 appear to indicate.

Following this release, it would seem that Paul toured the churches in Asia with Timothy and Titus. Leaving Timothy at Ephesus (1 Timothy 13) to take charge of the church and settle some of its internal problems, he proceeded to Crete and, after a short ministry, left Titus to shepherd the believers there (Titus 1:5). Both 1 Timothy and Titus appear to have been written during this period A.D. 64–66. From this evidence, it appears that Paul was arrested again and returned to Rome for confinement in prison, from which he wrote 2 Timothy, which is also dated A.D. 67–68. This letter indicates that he thought his death was imminent. In the light of this evidence, it is seen that these pastoral letters do not have to fit into the recorded events of the book of Acts.

The subject matter of these letters demands a vocabulary that would differ from the other Pauline letters. They show that the church, in its government and public worship, was developing and growing more complex, thus needing specific guidance in matters of church order. Such a change necessitated a different vocabulary from the earlier letters, which unfolded the great doctrines of the faith.

That these letters were written late in the apostolic age is evidenced not only by the complexity of church life, but also by the increased departure by the false teachers from the truth of God's Word. Heresy and error had increased, and the outbreak of rampant apostasy was increasingly imminent. These false teachers still claimed to be teachers of the law (1 Timothy 1:7) but they were urging men to "give heed to fables and endless genealogies" (1 Timothy 1:4). They professed to know God, but their very works denied him (Titus 1:16). Paul therefore brands them as corrupt in mind (1 Timothy 6:5), immoral (1 Timothy 4:3), and subverters of the faith (2 Timothy 2:17). Against such he warns both Timothy and Titus.

STUDY GUIDE OUTLINE TO THE PASTORAL LETTERS

1. **Ministry of the Pastorate** *1 Timothy*
   Pure doctrine for the Church *1*
   Public responsibilities of the Church *2*
   Prerequisites for Officers of the Church *3*
   Pastoral Pattern for the Church *4–6*
2. **Meditations Concerning the Pastorate** *2 Timothy*
   Persuasions of Paul *1*
   Pathway of Service *2*
   Prediction of Apostasy *3*
   Preparedness for Death *4*
3. **Management of the Pastorate** *Titus*
   Appointment to the Pastorate *1*
   Administration of the Pastorate *2*
   Affirmations for the Pastorate *3*

The purpose of the letters is to help two young pastors, very precious to Paul, to carry on their pastoral responsibilities. Paul exhorts them to hold fast to the doctrine of the faith, to oppose steadfastly the false teachers, and to give attention to the needs of their flock, especially the aged and widowed.

In the first letter, Paul sheds light upon Timothy's life. He was a Greek, but his mother was a Jewess, and from her and his grandmother he early gained a knowledge of the Scriptures. Evidently a convert of Paul's ministry (1:2), he was a son, in the faith, of Paul. Probably of a timid nature, Timothy needed encouragement and counsel in performing the work of the pastorate in the difficult, and often dangerous, pagan city of Ephesus.

The purpose of the second letter is clearly stated in 2 Timothy 4:9: "Do thy diligence to come shortly to me." Its theme forms a series of warnings and exhortations to Timothy as he performs the arduous duties and tasks associated with the pastorate of the Ephesian church. He is warned that the days are growing exceedingly perilous (3:1) and many are departing from the faith. He also has a sense that his own martyrdom is imminent (4:6–7), and thus is exhorted to "hold fast the form of sound words . . ." (1:13).

Titus, a Gentile brought to Christ under Paul's ministry, was a trusted companion and co-labourer of the apostle. As a co-worker of Paul, Titus had two most trying and difficult pastoral assignments:

1. He was Paul's representative to the factious, and sometimes morally lax, Corinthians.

Roman slaves had to wear a badge like this. The Latin words mean: "If I escape, arrest me and send me back to my master." Onesimus was an escaped slave.

2. He was also pastoral overseer of the church in Crete—that island peopled by a barbarous, crude, and morally contemptible people.

The purpose of the letter is to set forth the necessary relationship between true doctrine and godly living which should manifest itself in both church conduct and daily life. The primary emphasis is upon proper pastoral management of the local church.

Philemon

One of the so-called prison letters of Paul, this letter was written by Paul from Rome to Philemon and to the church in his house. It was common in apostolic days for the church to meet in a believer's home. The letter, therefore, was written in A.D. 60.

The letter deals with a slave, Onesimus, who, escaping from Philemon, had fled to Rome. There he came in contact with Paul and had come to know Christ as Saviour. Having now found opportunity to return Onesimus to his master, the apostle commends him to Philemon's forgiving grace. If he has caused Philemon any material loss, Paul says, "Put that on my account" (verse 18). The apostle is confident that Philemon will do more than is asked and that Onesimus will be released to the higher indenture of service to Christ.

Paul's letter to Philemon reveals that slavery was one of the curses of the ancient world. It has been estimated that there were some sixty million slaves in the Roman Empire. Does this mean

> **STUDY GUIDE OUTLINE TO PHILEMON**
> 1. Paul's Communication *1–7*
> 2. Paul's Commendation *8–20*
> 3. Paul's Confidence *21–25*

that Paul condoned slavery? Hardly! He recognized it as an evil of that day which could only be dealt with as men came to Christ and practised the ethics of the Christian faith.

Hebrews

The general meaning and message of this letter to the Hebrews are obvious, yet its authorship, place of composition, and destination have created many problems for scholars to try to settle. The certainty of authorship and destination can never be determined. From the early days of the church until the present time, the consensus has been that, while the epistle's genuineness and canonicity cannot be doubted, the problem of authorship and destination must remain in doubt. Its dating, however, must be before the destruction of Jerusalem, for the temple was still in existence and its observances were still being continued. To denote this the present tense is used (8:4, 13; 9:4–9; 10:1–11; 13:10–11).

The purpose of the letter, however, is quite clear. It was written to encourage Jewish Christians to go on in the Christian faith and to warn them against the possibility of apostasy. This apostasy would have involved their renunciation of the Christian faith and a return to Judaism. To fulfil this purpose, the writer shows the superiority of the Christian faith in every area of comparison with the Old Testament economy. Building on the value and validity of the Old Testament for its own time and place in the plan of God, he goes on to demonstrate by a series of comparisons that, with the coming of Christ, all of these things had their fulfilment, completion, and perfection in him. The important word in this connection is "better." Like Melchisedec, Christ is the King-Priest (7:1–28), and his provision of salvation is so great that the recipients of the letter are frequently warned against the danger of neglecting or rejecting it (2:1–3; 6:1–20; 10:19–39).

To return to Judaism would be to take a step backwards in God's plan of revelation and redemption, and would entail apostasy. A four-fold argument, with appropriate digressions of exhortations, warnings, and comforts, establishes the writer's purpose of demonstrating Christ's superiority.

A replica of the Jewish high priest's breastplate. Jesus Christ is the King-Priest.

James

James belongs to a group commonly known as the catholic, or general, epistles (including 1 and 2 Peter, 1, 2, 3 John, and Jude). These are so called perhaps because of the generalized teachings they contain or because of the general character of the readers addressed. While the authorship of James has been disputed, there is no reason to disagree with conservative scholars who claim that the author is James, the brother of the Lord. The external evidence is not unusually strong until the fourth century in the West, but in Jerusalem and the Syrian churches it was acknowledged early. The internal evidence is quite strong, and the letter claims to be written by James, who is well known from other passages of Scripture (Acts 15:13–21; 21:17–25; Galatians 1:19; 2:9–10).

Though reared in the same home as the Lord, James did not become a believer until after the resurrection of Christ. His life after that, however, was so evidently dedicated to God and the living of a strict, disciplined life that he became known as James "the righteous." He presided "as one of the pillars of the church" at the first council of the church in Jerusalem (Acts 15). He is also mentioned as one of those who urged Paul to make a vow (Acts 21:18), as one of those seen by Paul during his visit to Jerusalem (Galatians 1:19), and as one named by Jude as his brother (Jude 1:1).

James addressed his letter "to the twelve tribes scattered abroad." It is thus Jewish in its designation, and those addressed were manifestly Jewish Christians who were believers from among the Jews of the dispersion. Those believers were still tied to Jewish traditions and customs. This would seem to point to an early date for the writing of the letter, and many scholars would contend that it was the earliest of all the letters of the New Testament. It was probably written some time between A.D. 45 and 50.

This letter was written to urge believers to demonstrate their justification by faith through their good works in the Christian life. Steadfastness in the Christian faith will provide the environment in which Christian virtues can develop, resulting in a properly balanced life of holiness. To James, there is such a thing as "pure religion and undefiled before God and the Father . . ." (1:27). There needs to be a reality to religion, a faith backed up by a good life, and a creed validated by conduct.

STUDY GUIDE OUTLINE TO JAMES

1. The Perfection of Faith *1:1–2:13*
2. The Product of Faith *2:14–26*
3. The Problem of Faith *3:1–12*
4. The Proofs of Faith *3:13–5:6*
5. The Patience of Faith *5:7–20*

1 & 2 Peter

The profile of Israel's Mount Tabor is unmistakable. Tradition has it that it was the site of Jesus' transfiguration.

It would seem that the New Testament would be incomplete without some writings from the hand of Peter, the disciple so intimately associated with the Lord Jesus. Even though most scholars believe that Mark was indebted to Peter for his gospel, this would not satisfy the desire to have writings from Peter.

These two letters come from Peter, and the truths revealed in them are in keeping with that intimacy which Peter had with Christ. Thus, it is not out of order to call them precious truths, as Peter himself did: "That the trial of your faith, being much more precious than of gold that perisheth . . ." (1 Peter 1:7). Speaking of our redemption, he writes, "But with the precious blood of Christ . . ." (1 Peter 1:19). Of Christ, as chief cornerstone, he quotes the prophet, "Behold, I lay in Zion a chief cornerstone, elect, precious . . ." (1 Peter 2:6). And he reminds us of the preciousness of Christ, "Unto you therefore which believe he is precious . . ." (1 Peter 2:7).

That Peter was the author of the first letter has abundant and strong support from evidence both external and internal. Beginning with quotes from it by Polycarp and a direct naming of it by Irenaeus, the universal testimony of the early church is that Peter wrote it. The internal evidence shows that the writer calls himself Peter (1:1) and that he was intimately acquainted with Christ: he witnessed Christ's sufferings (5:1; compare 3:18; 4:1); he notes

STUDY GUIDE OUTLINE TO 1 & 2 PETER

1. The Privileges of Believers in Christ *1 Peter*
   a. Salvation in Christ *1:1–2:10*
   b. Submission Through Christ *2:11–4:11*
   c. Service for Christ *4:12–5:14*

2. The Promises to Believers in Christ *2 Peter*
   a. Power of Christ *1*
   b. Preservation by Christ *2*
   c. Prediction Concerning Christ's Return *3*

the Person of Christ in his sufferings (2:19–24); and he uses statements that allude to some of Christ's actions (5:5 compare with John 13:3–5; and 5:2 compare with John 21:15–17). There are no adequate reasons to deny Peter's authorship.

Both Paul and Peter, according to tradition, were martyred in Rome during Nero's persecution (A.D. 67–68). This would mean then that Peter wrote this letter from Rome (if "Babylon" is taken as a mystic name for Rome as many believe) about A.D. 65.

The first letter was written to the believers in Pontus, Galatia, Cappadocia, Asia, and Bithynia. That Paul founded the churches in Galatia and Asia is evident, but there is no evidence that either Paul or Peter had ever visited the other provinces (Acts 16:7). Perhaps converts of Paul may have founded these churches, or they were founded by early converts from Jerusalem (Acts 2:9–10). In any case, the believers were from among both Jews and Gentiles.

The believers were suffering certain trials and hardships, even though there was no organized persecution against them. They were, however, undergoing a subtle and more severe kind of difficulty. They were experiencing the suffering of a world hostile to their faith. They were being slandered and vilified and, as a result, some were experiencing the loss of goods and imminent ruin.

The purpose of the letter is to comfort and encourage these believers to stand steadfastly in the "true grace of God" (5:12) in a world that hated them and their testimony. Holding up the sufferings of Christ as an example for believers (1:11; 2:21, 23; 4:1–2; 5:1) and using some severe words for suffering, he writes this letter as a word of hope in the midst of suffering. He reminds them that God has begotten them unto a living hope (1 Peter 1:3).

The second letter of Peter has not fared as well as his first letter when it comes to the question of authorship. Because of the

difference in vocabulary, and a certain awkwardness of style, many have doubted Peter's authorship. The external evidence for the letter as Peter's is somewhat weak, but the internal evidence is quite strong. The references to his life and events mentioned in the letter give sufficient testimony that Peter was the author. There is mention of such significant events as his approaching death (1:13), the transfiguration of Christ (1:16–18), and the sending of a previous letter (3:1). Moreover, in certain grammatical features (for example, the use of the article) 1 and 2 Peter are more alike than any other two New Testament epistles.

This letter, like Paul's second letter to Timothy, was the benediction of Peter. It was written towards the close of his life (1:13), and expresses his grave concern about the deepening shadows of apostasy. Reckless living characterized those who were false teachers, and preceding it went the denial of certain cherished doctrines, such as God's revelation in the Bible (1:19–21), and the doctrine of the Lord's return (3:9–10).

The major emphasis of this letter is upon knowledge (3:18). The words "know" and "knowledge" are used frequently, and the admonition to grow in the knowledge of Christ will enable them to combat the errors of false teachers concerning the Lord's return. The purpose, therefore, of the letter was to warn his readers against false teachers and teaching and to encourage them concerning the truth of the Lord's return. This is done by speaking of the promises which had been given to them in Christ.

The landscape of Cappadocia is remarkable. First Peter was written to believers in Pontus, Galatia, Cappadocia, Asia, and Bithynia.

1, 2 & 3 John

Aegean Sea

PATMOS

The author of 1, 2, and 3 John is John, the well-known and beloved disciple of the Lord Jesus. He might be termed the Elder Statesman. His life, though arduous and filled with many instances of difficulty, such as his exile on the Isle of Patmos, was a good life, and he lived, tradition states, until he was about one hundred years old. John wrote these letters, as well as the gospel which bears his name, and the book of Revelation, towards the close of his long and fruitful life. These letters were written, therefore, after the destruction of Jerusalem, and thus are to be dated between A.D. 85 and 90.

The writings of John are deeply spiritual, personal, profound, and loving. The relationship of John to the Lord Jesus was one of deep devotion and dedication, and he was known as the disciple who leaned on Jesus' breast. As such, he possessed a mystical nature and placed great emphasis on the principle of love. Yet one cannot think of John as either weak-willed or purely sentimental. He could speak of God's great love (John 3:16) but also God's wrath and condemnation (John 3:36). This shows that his love was not merely emotional but grounded in the holiness and righteousness of God.

John wrote his gospel to prove Christ's deity, assuming throughout Christ's humanity (John 20:30–31). In the letters, he wrote to prove Christ's humanity, assuming Christ's deity throughout (1 John 1:1). This emphasis shows that early Gnosticism was a problem to the believers, and they needed instruction. Gnosticism

---

STUDY GUIDE OUTLINE TO 1, 2 & 3 JOHN

1. Fellowship of Love *1 John*
    The Manifestation of Fellowship–God is Light *1–2*
    The Manner of Fellowship–God is Holy *3:1–4:6*
    The Motive for Fellowship–God is Love *4:7–5:21*

2. Faithfulness in Love *2 John*
    The Commendation for Faithfulness *1–4*
    The Commandment to Faithfulness *5–6*
    The Counsel Concerning Faithfulness *7–11*
    The Commitment to Faithfulness *12–13*

3. Frankness of Love *3 John*
    The Responsible One–Gaius *1–8*
    The Rebellious One—Diotrephes *9–10*
    The Respected One—Demetrius *11–12*

considered matter as evil, and thus Christ could not have a human body. Thus, their Docetism (which taught that Christ only appeared or seemed to have a body, from *dokeo* "to appear," "to seem") had to be confronted. Gnosticism also taught that only by knowledge (*gnosis*) could one get from the world of material, or evil, to spirit, which is good. Thus John emphasized, in contradistinction, the true knowledge or great certainties of the Christian faith, which alone can save us. Note the frequent use of "know" in this first letter, where John uses it more than twenty-five times.

The purpose of John is also to show that Christ is the believer's Advocate, while his adversary is the anti-christ and the antichristian system. The believer is not to love the world but to love fellow believers and walk in the light, as God is in the light (1 John 1:1–2:23). The believer is to walk in holiness and love, as God is holy and loving (1 John 3:1–5:21).

The second letter of John reveals the pastoral heart of the beloved apostle. It is not certain whether it is addressed to an individual woman or a local church. But regardless, it reveals the pastor's familiarity with the life and work of God's children. John urges faithfulness on their part to the truth.

The third letter is a study in three personalities and reflects through them some of the conditions of the early church. These three people reveal the personal responsibility of individual members to the work of the local church. The governing motive should be, but is not always, devotion to the lordship of Christ. This is a study of Christian character.

The isle of Patmos in the Aegean. John was exiled on this little island.

Jude

There is such a striking similarity in style, thought, and purpose between 2 Peter and Jude that many scholars have felt that one copied from the other. Other scholars, such as Tenney, feel that Jude saw Peter's letter and was stimulated to write this letter.

Though having stronger external evidence for its authorship than 2 Peter, there has been disagreement as to which Jude wrote it. There seems, however, no reason to doubt that it was Jude the brother of James, and the half-brother of Jesus (Mark 6:3). Like his brother James (Jude 1), he probably did not come to trust Christ until after the resurrection.

Some believe that this letter was written to the church in Jerusalem and date it after Peter's letters, about A.D. 66–68. Others, believing that verse 17 probably refers to Peter's prediction of the coming apostasy, and thus Peter's letter was already in circulation, date the letter between A.D. 75 and 80, because of Jude's description of the apostate teachers who seem to be well-known and whose influence was being felt in the churches. This later date would allow time for the development of the apostasy.

The occasion and purpose of the letter are not hard to find. Jude gives them to us in verse 3. The presence of apostasy had called forth a delineation of its nature, a demand to combat it, and an exhortation to persevere in the true faith. The theme of the letter is the preservation of the Christian faith, both as to its content and as to its conduct in the lives of believers.

STUDY GUIDE OUTLINE TO JUDE

1. Preamble to Apostasy *1–2*
2. Problem of Apostasy *3–7*
3. Pride of the Apostates *8–16*
4. Prediction Concerning Apostasy *17–19*
5. Provisions Against Apostasy *20–25*

Revelation

The author of Revelation is the same person who wrote the gospel and the three letters that bear his name. It is John, the "beloved apostle," and the one who leaned on Jesus' breast (John 13:25) and who was now on the Isle of Patmos in the Aegean Sea because of his testimony for the faith. Whilst there, he received from Christ a series of visions so that he might be able to give to the church the prophetic programme of God for the consummation of human history. The book reveals that God's hand is upon the human scene, and he is directing it towards a final goal. The external and internal evidence is strong for John's authorship (1:1, 4, 9; 21:2; 22:8).

The book belongs to a type of literature which is called apocalyptic. It is so named because it was written during times of persecution and suffering to give encouragement and hope, signs and symbols are used, and the idea of judgment to vindicate God's plans and purpose is frequently included. This book of Revelation differs from the general body of such literature in that it was not written under an assumed name. The author of the book is known, and he was also well-known during the time that the visions took place and the book was written.

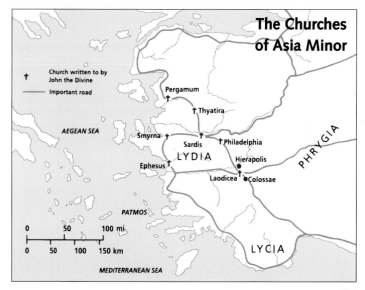

STUDY GUIDE OUTLINE TO REVELATION

1. Revelation of Christ to John *1*
2. Remarks of Christ to the Churches *2–3*
3. Retribution of Christ upon the World *4–18*
4. Return of Christ to the World *19:1–20:6*
5. Rejection of Christ by the World *20:7–15*
6. Rewards of Christ to the Believers *21–22*

There is some disagreement as to the exact date of this book's writing. There are those who place it during the reign of the monstrous and incorrigible Nero (A.D. 64–65). This appears too early a date, for the history and circumstances of the churches addressed in the book show a development that could not have taken place in such a short period of history. The book thus could not have been written much earlier than the later date usually assigned to it. This is the reign of Domitian, which was another time of severe persecution for the Christian church. This would place the writing of the book at the close of the first century, about A.D. 96.

Interpreters differ as to the method of interpretation to be used to ascertain the meaning and message of the book. There are four methods advanced:

1. The spiritual, which believes that the book deals with the conflict between the church and evil forces through the entire history of the church.

2. The praeterist, or past, which teaches that the greater part of the book has already been fulfilled.

3. The continuous-historical, which states that throughout the church's history the book is being fulfilled, until the consummation of history with the coming again of Christ.

4. The futurist, which notes that the first three chapters have already been fulfilled (though some teach that the seven churches give a prophetic history of the church until the coming of Christ) and that chapters 4–22 are still future.

Regarding the interpretation of the tribulation (6:16–17; 7:14) there are three views:

1. Pre-tribulation, which holds that believers will be raptured before the seven-year period of tribulation (Daniel's seventieth week, Daniel 9:27).

2. Mid-tribulation, which states that believers will be raptured at the end of the first three and a half years (11:1–19).

3. Post-tribulation, which states that believers will go through the entire seven-year period of tribulation (19:11–21).

It should be noted that although these views are at variance, they all operate within Pre-millennial teaching (20:1–10).

In chapter 20, John speaks of a period of one thousand years of the millennium. Various interpretations are given of this period:

1. The amillennial view, which denies any literal millennial period, and states that it is only a spiritual period which began with Satan's binding at the death and resurrection of Christ and will end with Christ's cataclysmic coming to consummate human history.

2. The postmillennial view, that holds the gospel will ultimately bring righteousness throughout the earth, and, at the end of one thousand years of such world-embracing righteousness, Christ will come and usher in the eternal, heavenly state.

3. The pre-millennial view, that teaches that Christ will return and establish the millennial kingdom on earth over the nations, and, after Satan's final rebellion at the end of the millennium, this kingdom will blend into the eternal kingdom of God (1 Corinthians 15:23–28).

Part of the meagre remains of Laodicea, the church that was warned of its lukewarmness.

Index

Page numbers in *italics* denote illustrations.